# A GARDEN OF MEDICINAL PLANTS

First published in Great Britain in 2015 by Little, Brown

Picture credits: Pages 16 (far left), 19, 45, 48 © Jonathan Perugia. Page 20 © Helene Binet Page 124 © Simon Williams. Page 128 © Nick Hufton. All other pictures © Henry Oakeley.

Designed by Emil Dacanay and Sian Rance, D.R. ink

A CIP catalogue record for this book is available from the British Library.

ISBN 978-1-4087-0624-4

Printed and bound in China

# 500
## REFLECTIONS
## ON THE RCP
## 1518–2018

# A GARDEN OF
# MEDICINAL PLANTS

## Jane Knowles
## Anthony Dayan
## Michael de Swiet
## Henry Oakeley

Royal College
of Physicians

# FOREWORD

The Royal College of Physicians was founded, by Royal Charter, in 1518 by King Henry VIII. Few professional organisations have been in continuous existence for so long, and over its five-hundred-year history the College has been at the centre of many aspects of medical life. Its purpose is to promote the highest standards of medical practice in order to improve health and health care, and its varied work in the field is held in very high regard. Currently, the College has over thirty thousand members and fellows worldwide. Over the years it has accumulated a distinguished library, extensive archives, museum collections of portraits and other treasures, and has been housed in a number of notable buildings. As part of its quincentennial commemoration, a series of ten books has been commissioned, of which this is the second part. Each book features fifty items, thereby making a total of five hundred, and the series is intended to be a meditation on, and an exploration of, aspects of the College's work and collections over its five-hundred-year history.

This, the second volume of the series, focuses on the College's medicinal garden, which is as the authors put it 'a living museum of the history of medicine and medicines'. The book celebrates what is an extraordinary garden, and is academic, original, authoritative and readable. It is a fascinating survey of a fascinating topic.

*Simon Shorvon -*

**Simon Shorvon, Harveian Librarian, Royal College of Physicians**
**Series Editor**

5

6 | 5OO REFLECTIONS ON THE RCP

# CONTENTS

# A GARDEN OF MEDICINAL PLANTS

The Medicinal Garden of the Royal College of Physicians is 'the most interesting garden in London'. It is a living museum of the history of medicine and medicines, a unique pedagogic institution to demonstrate the plants used in medicines by our predecessors and those which still make a substantial contribution to our health. The Garden covers all disciplines: there are the plants used by the College physicians in our early years, made famous by our *Pharmacopoeia Londinensis* of 1618, many of which were used by contemporary herbalists, some used as the source of medicines which pre-date the pyramids of Egypt, and others which have given rise to modern pharmaceuticals. Some have caused sickness and medical disasters and others commemorate early physicians. The disciplines of Ayurvedic and Traditional Chinese Medicine are only slightly represented, due to the limitations posed by the English climate. Our herbarium, originally from the Royal Pharmaceutical Society, has 5800 historic specimens dating back to 1795 from every continent to compensate for this lack. While the emphasis is on our European heritage, the Garden has plants from the medical tradition of Native Americans, 'Muthi' medicine used by 30 million people in South Africa, plants from Ancient Greece and Rome, Europe and the Middle East, as well as representative taxa from Asia, South America, Australia, the Pacific Islands and the arid regions of the world. In commemoration of that great Greek philosopher we have the Socratic Garden, where we grow hemlock, *Conium maculatum*, and other famous poisons. Toxicity is a feature of most plants, from apple pips to deadly nightshade, as a useful evolutionary device to avoid extinction in the maws of herbivores and insects, so even in the main Garden few are edible.

> **There are the plants used as the source of medicines which pre-date the pyramids of Egypt and others which have given rise to modern pharmaceuticals.**

This book starts with a history of the Garden and then, as space does not permit us to describe every one of the approximately 1100 plants, we concentrate on some of those whose impact over the long span of past centuries have been the most significant. From time to time we will expand our theme to detail the history, discovery, chemistry, therapeutic uses, etc., of a plant, with references to point the reader towards the concept of evidence-based science and medicine and further reading. For other plants, we relate the documented history of their medicinal use as far back as the Trojan Wars of 1200BCE, and debunk a few myths. The assiduous reader will miss some well-known plants, but we hope we will be forgiven for our selection.

# CURRENT *DRAMATIS PERSONAE*

### The Gardeners
Head Gardener: Jane Knowles
Assistant Gardeners:
Sam Crosfield, Clare Beacham (2007–2014)
### The Garden Fellows
Dr Henry Oakeley
Prof Michael de Swiet
Prof Anthony Dayan
Prof John Newton

### Literary *Dramatis Personae*
The importance of primary source references for early beliefs and uses cannot be overstated, and the historic herbals in the Dorchester Library are a valuable resource. These are the main authors of historic herbals whose writings are referenced in this book.

The modern references have been omitted from the text because of space considerations. All the supercript references can be retrieved on-line at https://www.rcplondon.ac.uk/medicinalgardenbook

Anglicus, Bartholomeus (ca.1203–72) wrote *De proprietatibus rerum* in 1240, published in 1492.

Anglicus, Gilbertus (ca.1180–1250) English physician whose *Compendium Medicinae* (1510) was a summary of English medicine and surgery, based on Galen, Hippocrates, Avicenna and many others. No direct references used. Appears as the doctor in Chaucer. See Henderson.[24]

Apuleius, also known as Pseudo-Apuleius, author of the influential C4 herbal, *Herbarium Apuleii Platonici*, based on Pliny and Dioscorides. Contains 130 plants with uses and synonyms. We use Hummelberger's *De Medicaminibus Herbarum* edition of 1537, the first printing from northern Europe.

Thomas Linacre, first President of the College, looks out over the Garden

Henry Pierrepont, Marquess of Dorchester, who gave us his library in 1687–8

Avicenna, an Arabian physician in Baghdad whose *Canon of Medicine* (*Quanun* V1.11), ca.1020, was based on Greek texts, translated into Syriac in ca. 1500 by Nestorian Christians in Persia, and later into Arabic, enshrining medical knowledge at the end of the first millennium until ca. 1650.

Cordus, Valerius (1515–44). German physician, botanist. His *Dispensatorium* (aka *Pharmacorum omnium,* 1546), completed when aged twenty-seven, published posthumously, was a compilation of existing compound medicines adopted by the city of Nuremburg. It became the basis for pharmacopoeias for the next hundred years, including our own *Pharmacopoeia Londinensis* (May 1618).

Culpeper, Nicholas (1616–54). English herbalist and physician who translated the second edition of the *Pharmacopoeia Londinensis* (December 1618) into English, adding in the uses of the plants and medicines, sourced widely from classical and contemporary authors. We use this, his *Physical Directory* (1649 – second edition 1650), with short simple entries throughout.

Dioscorides, Pedanius of Anazarbus (40–90CE). Greek physician from Cecilia. All Dioscorides references are to his *Materia Medica* of ca. 70CE containing the uses of about 600 plants. This was the basis for medicine for nearly 1700 years; Beck (2005) and Gunther (1959) are the two English translations used. For commentaries we mainly use the Latin editions of Matthiolus (1558, 1569, 1586) and Ruel (1537, 1543) with their numerous woodcuts.

Dodoens, Rembert (1517–85). Flemish physician and botanist; he wrote his ground-breaking *Cruydeboeck* in 1554 on the medicinal uses of plants, in Flemish, with 715 woodcuts. He translated it into Latin for a wider audience as *Stirpium Historiae Pemptades Sex* (1583). Other translations (*q.v.*) by L'Escluse (1577), Lyte (1578) and Gerard (1597).

Fernel (Fernelius), Jean (1497–1558). A French cosmologist, mathematician and physician to Catherine de' Medici. We use the 1593 edition (first edition, 1569) of his *Therapeutices Universalis*, one of the three great pharmacopoeias of the sixteenth century, with Occo's *Augustana* and Cordus's *Dispensatorium.*

Fuchs, Leonard or Leonhart (1501–66). German physician and botanist. His herbal, *De Historia Stirpium commentarii insignes* (1542, Notable commentaries on the history of plants), set a new standard in woodcut illustrations. He quotes Galen, Dioscorides, Paulus Aegineta and Pliny for their uses. Small octavo edition in 1551.

Galen, Claudius of Pergamon (129–ca.200/216). Greek physician, surgeon in Rome, who was the dominant medical authority until the seventeenth century. No source book used; references from Fuchs (1542), Parkinson (1640) and others.

**Gerard, John** (1545–1612). Herbalist, surgeon and gardener, he published the monumental *Herball, or Generall Historie of Plantes* in 1597 using the English translation (1583) of Rembert Dodoens done by a Dr Priest of the College of the Latin *Pemptades*. L'Obel helped sort out the many errors. We have used Thomas Johnson's revised edition of 1633 with 2766 woodblocks.

**Hippocrates** (468–377BCE). The 'father of medicine' and of the Doctrine of the Humours. No primary text used.

**L'Escluse, Charles de** (1526–1609). A Flemish doctor who translated Dodoens' *Cruydeboeck* into French as *Histoire des Plantes* (1577).

**Lyte, Henry** (1529–1607) translated L'Escluse's *Histoire des Plantes* (1577) into English as *Nievve herball* or *historie of plantes* (1578) in black letter font, with 870 woodcuts, and his own opinions added. A rare but useful source with significant differences from Gerard.

**Matthiolus (Mattioli), Pierandrea** (1501–77). Born in Sienna, physician to Archduke Ferdinand and Maximillian II. Prolific publisher; his *Commentarii … de Materia Medica* of Dioscorides sold tens of thousands of copies. We use the editions of 1554, 1558, 1569 and his *De Plantis Epitome* of 1558.

**Occo III, Adolphus** (1524–1606). The third of a four-generation dynasty of German physicians, he was Augsburg's city physician, inspector of its apothecary shops and compiler of its pharmacopoeia, the *Pharmacopoeia Augustana* (1564). Latter based on Cordus's *Dispensatorium* (1546).

**Parkinson, John** (1567–1650). Apothecary to James I and botanist to Charles I, he wrote the most inclusive English herbal of all, *Theatrum Botanicum*, in 1640. It contained 3800 plants with detailed (often confused) reviews of the writings of earlier authors, with woodcuts.

**Pliny Secundus**, or Pliny the Elder (23CE–79CE). Roman philosopher, naturalist. He compiled the encyclopaedic *Naturalis Historia* (Natural History) in ca. 77CE, and all Pliny references are to the magnificent English translation by Philemon Holland of 1644.

**Ruel, Jean** (1474–1537). French physician, botanist, whose Latin translation of Dioscorides was used by Matthiolus. His commentaries on Dioscorides and woodcuts are less extensive than those of Matthiolus. We use the edition of 1543 and his *De Natura Stirpium* (On the Nature of Plants, 1537).

**Theophrastus** (371–287BCE), a Greek philosopher, physician, 'father of botany', author of *Historia Plantarum,* Enquiry into Plants. We use Scaliger's Latin edition of 1644.[62]

# THE HISTORY OF THE GARDEN

## BY JANE KNOWLES

enys Lasdun's design for the new home of the RCP featured a quarter-acre plot for making a garden and this meant that for the first time in 140 years the College's headquarters had some outside space. Previous homes, notably Amen Corner (1614–66) and Warwick Lane (1674–1825), had had small plots, but despite attempts over the years to create 'a repository of simples', or medicinal plants, there is no evidence that these gardens were ever more than recreational spaces. The most tantalising glimpse of what might have been comes in a note in the College annals of an approach in 1587 to John Gerard (1545–1612), the surgeon plantsman and author of the great *Herball* of 1597. He was offered a paid position to look after the College Garden: a garden which, due to lack of evidence to the contrary, we must assume never materialised.

Four hundred and fifty years after the College was founded, Dr W. Copeman left a bequest for the planting of a new garden around the Lasdun building. He stipulated the planting of at least two medicinal plants: a Willow (source of the salicylates much used in his speciality of rheumatology) and a Castor Oil Plant (castor oil being the remedy commonly associated with physicians of his generation). The first request was honoured and we still grow a representative of this genus; the second was more problematic as the source of Castor Oil, *Ricinus communis*, is a tender plant from East Africa which the contractors in charge found impractical to

*Ricinus.*

ABOVE: Woodcut of *Ricinus communis*, the Castor oil plant and source of ricin, from Lobel's herbal, *Plantarum seu Stirpium Historia*, of 1576
OPPOSITE: The Japanese flowering cherry, *Prunus serrulata* var. *longipes* 'Shimidsu Sakura' in the College Garden, April 2009, with the gardeners, L–R Jane Knowles and Clare Beacham

Original plants in the Garden
TOP LEFT: *Drimys winteri*
ABOVE: *Salix chaenomeloides*
RIGHT: *Halesia carolina*

grow. False Castor Oil, *Fatsia japonica*, was planted instead and, although it has no medicinal value, it still flourishes at the back of a border here. We do now grow *Ricinus communis* among many other exotic species.

The most significant plant from these early years is the magnificent *Platanus orientalis* (see page 21), planted in 1969 to commemorate Hippocrates (468–377BCE), the father of medicine. He taught his students beneath Oriental plane trees on the island of Cos and this specimen is a descendant of an ancient tree from that island.

In 1977 Dr Arthur Hollman, the renowned cardiologist with an interest in the history of medicine and a passion for plants, took on responsibility for the Garden. He put in plants which were relevant to the College and to the practice of medicine. Several significant trees and some shrubs remain to provide the Garden with a lovely mature framework. They include *Drimys winteri*, Winter's Bark, a South American tree rich in vitamin C and used by Captain John Winter (who sailed in 1577 with Francis Drake on his circumnavigation of the globe) to treat his crew who were suffering from scurvy. Also *Halesia carolina*, planted in 1977 to commemorate the Reverend Dr Stephen Hales (1677–1761), the first person to measure blood pressure and sap pressure.

Another of Dr Hollman's plants is the Pomegranate, *Punica granatum*, planted in 1977 (see page 44). The fruit is on the College's coat of arms and has a long history of use as a medicinal plant, mostly for gastroenterological complaints. It also carries cultural and religious significance, being associated with regeneration, the persistence of life and fertility.

In 1986 the College acquired the adjacent Regency terrace of 1 to 10 St Andrews Place and with it eight front gardens and the plot at the top of the existing lawn. The front gardens remained as eight small lawns while the adjoining plot was landscaped to join the rest of the garden, with paths and beds laid out to a plan by Denys Lasdun. The layout is still much as he conceived it and the total area now, as then, covers three-quarters of an acre. Following this Dr Hollman retired and there was a move to make the gardens more decorative. Different designers were consulted, including Penelope Hobhouse, who planted the box parterre at the front. This geometric design with straight lines and square form, to echo and balance the building, is the main feature remaining from this period.

In 2004 the redevelopment of the gardens as a collection of medicinal plants began under the aegis of the then Treasurer and later President of the College, Sir Richard Thompson. He enlisted the help of Dr Henry Oakeley and they invited Mark Griffiths, writer and garden designer, to redesign and re-plant the garden. His concept was 'to create a new physic garden for the 21st century … to reflect different traditions of medicine and to demonstrate plants of established and more recently determined clinical significance'. Additional funding was provided by a grant from the Wolfson Foundation and this initial stage began in 2004 and ran through to the beginning of 2006. The tired and overgrown borders at the back and front of the College were cleared and restocked with some 600 species of plant, all with a link to medicine. At the end of 2005 I became Head Gardener and Clare Beacham joined me as Assistant in 2007. We continued planting and now have over 1100 different species, all recorded on a database http://garden.rcplondon.ac.uk .

Penelope Hobhouse's box parterre

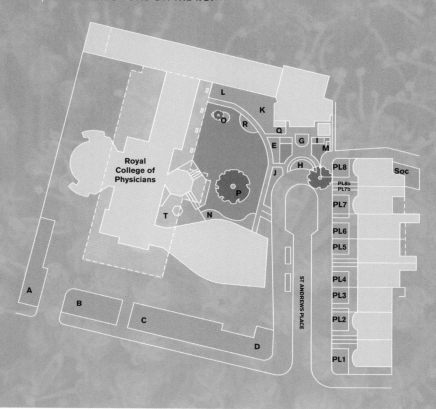

Royal
College of
Physicians

ST ANDREWS PLACE

**A** North American bed

**B,C,D** World medicine beds

**PL1–8** *Pharmacopoeia Londinensis* beds

   **1** Flowers

   **2** Roots

   **3** Roots

   **4** Fruit

   **5** Leaves

   **6** Leaves

   **7** Seeds and grains

   **7b** Bark and wood

   **8** Seeds and grains

   **8b** Gums and resin

**E** European and Mediterranean beds

**G** Box horseshoe

**H** Mulberry bed

**I** Classical world bed

**J** European and Middle Eastern beds

**K** Southern hemisphere bed

**L** Oriental bed

**M** Classical European and Middle Eastern bed

**N** Southern hemisphere bed

**O** Olive tree bed

**P** Hippocratic plane tree

**Q** Arid zone

**R** Display bed

**T** Terrace

**Soc** Socratic garden

The Lasdun building is now surrounded on three sides by flower beds or lawn. The majority of the planting in the back garden is arranged according to the geographical origins of the plants. The front beds are more mixed: the 'world medicine beds'. The eight front gardens along the precinct of St Andrews Place were re-planted in 2006 as a living representation of the plants listed in the College's first *Pharmacopoeia Londinensis* of 1618 (its publication marking another memorable date, the College's first centenary).

Everything we plant now has a story to tell about medicine. The plants might have been used by another culture, in another time, or be the source of an important pharmaceutical or even named after a doctor. We aim to celebrate all the many ways in which health, life and death are, and always have been, dependent on our knowledge of plants.

**We aim to celebrate all the many ways in which health, life and death are, and always have been, dependent on our knowledge of plants.**

ABOVE: Jane Knowles collecting seeds of the Corn Poppy. *Papaver rhoeas*
OPPOSITE: The front gardens of St Andrews Place house the plants used as medicines in the College's *Pharmacopoeia Londinensis* of 1618

# PLANTS FROM THE BEGINNING OF TIME

Some plants have been associated with medicine, or used as medicines, since the era of the Ancient Greeks and their Roman successors. These have a place in the College Garden so we do not forget our distinguished history or the long story of how plants have been used for their effect on our bodies, for good and ill.

## PLATANUS ORIENTALIS SUBSP. INSULARIS

**Platanus orientalis** subsp. **insularis L.** or *Platanus insularis* Kotschy ex Koehne. Platanaceae. Oriental plane. Distribution: Greek Islands.

his tall tree in the College lawn commemorates Hippocrates, the Father of Medicine, who taught his medical students in 400BCE under a plane tree on the island of Cos, off the coast of mainland Greece. There is a huge tree there, about 500 years old, with a diameter of 12 metres, which bears a sign that it is the original tree. While there are no plane trees 2500 years old, it may well, however, be a descendant. Seed from this tree was taken to the National Botanic Garden in New York by the distinguished Canadian neurosurgeon Wilder Penfield. Cuttings

from the resulting seedlings were sent to the Royal Botanic Gardens, Kew, and from there one was donated to the Royal College of Physicians, London, in 1965. A second tree, which came from the same source via the Chelsea Physic Garden, was also planted in the College lawn in 1965, but removed after a number of years. The surviving tree has vast superficial roots which snake across the lawn, so will never be a suitable tree for street planting. In the summer it provides welcome shade and is under-planted with wild flowers to attract insects and other wildlife. As winter gives way to spring it hosts a vast carpet of golden winter aconites, *Eranthis hyemalis*.

ABOVE: Winter Aconites, under the plane tree

TOP: *Papaver somniferum*, the Opium Poppy
ABOVE: Flower of *Papaver somniferum* the
Opium poppy, being pollinated

# PAPAVER SOMNIFERUM

**Papaver somniferum** L. Papaveraceae. Opium Poppy. Distribution: Asia Minor.

his is our oldest effective medicine in continuous use, described in the Ebers Papyrus, dated 1550BCE. Remains in Spanish cave dwellings, dated to 5000BCE, indicate an even longer pedigree. It now grows almost everywhere, from the Andes of Peru to the United States of America, from war-torn Afghanistan to suburban Britain. It shares its medicinal properties with other members of the genus *Papaver*, all of which have been used to make medicines, with historic names such as Meconium, Laudanum, Paregoric and Syrup of Poppies. Culpeper writes that Meconium is '…the juyce of English Poppies [*Papaver rhoeas*] boyled till it be thick' and hazards the correct guess: 'I am of the opinion that Opium is nothing else but the juyce of poppies growing in hotter countries, *for such Opium as Authors talk of comes from Utopia.*' He cautions 'Syrups of Poppies provoke sleep, but in that I desire they may be used with a great deal of caution and wariness …' and warns in particular against giving syrup of poppies to children to get them to sleep.

The sap of *Papaver somniferum* is known as opium. It contains various alkaloids including morphine (12%), which affect μ-opioid receptors in the brain and elsewhere, producing happiness, sleepiness, pain relief, cough suppression and constipation. It is harvested by making incisions into the green seedpod and collecting the sap after it has dried. The volume of fresh sap that would cover the tip of a small penknife tastes horrible but is sufficient to cause a transient mental relaxation and dream-like state twenty minutes later. A whole seed head would be an opiate overdose – the strength (and toxicity) of plant-sourced medicines are not to be underestimated. The sap also contains codeine (3%) which has mild opiate actions after conversion to morphine in the body. Not all opiates are analgesic: another constituent is papaverine, which relaxes smooth muscle spasm in the arteries of the heart and brain and so has been used to treat angina and cerebral aneurysms, with additional uses for intestinal spasm, migraine and erectile dysfunction. Thebaine, another opiate which is mildly analgesic and stimulatory, is made into oxycodone and oxymorphone, which are powerful synthetic analgesics. A small percentage of protopine, an analgesic antihistamine which relieves the pain of inflammation is also present, as well as noscapine, which is used to suppress coughing.

In 2006 the world production of opium was 6,610 metric tons; in 1906 it was over 30,000 tons when 25% of Chinese males were regular users. The opium wars of the nineteenth century were caused by Britain selling huge quantities of opium to China. We can no longer obtain Laudanum (10mg of morphine (as opium) per ml) but Gee's Linctus and Kaolin and Morph which contain small amounts of morphine are still available across the counter without prescription. Heroin is made from morphine, but is converted back into morphine in the body. One gram of poppy seeds contains 0.25mg morphine, and while one poppy seed bagel will make a urine test positive for morphine for a week (and be detectable in hair for up to nine months), one would need twenty to thirty bagels to have any discernible opiate effect.

# CONIUM MACULATUM

**Conium maculatum** L. Apiaceae. Hemlock. Distribution: Europe.

 emlock, a wayside plant from the Cow Parsley family with its mottled (*maculatum*) stems, is famous for being responsible for the death of Socrates (469–399BCE). We grow it in the Socratic Garden, our secret, locked garden in Peto Place, the home for our most poisonous plants.

Since the earliest times it has been known to be very toxic to man and animals, although not to birds, causing death by producing paralysis and a cold feeling ascending from the feet that is fatal when it reaches the chest and respiration fails. It also causes incoordination, thirst and sometimes convulsions. It was used by the Greeks and Romans to execute prisoners, most notably Socrates, as related in Plato's *Phaedo*. It was mixed with opium and taken with wine to ensure a speedier and less troublesome death. Poisoning may follow contact with the sap so thick gloves should be worn when handling the plant.

The toxic chemicals are piperidine alkaloids present throughout the plant, mainly coniine, which resist cooking. Coniine blocks cholinergic muscle receptors and inhibits neural signalling systems. There is no known antidote. Garrod (1886) notes that the vapour of heated coniine has been used to relieve cough, including whooping cough (pertussis), and asthma, and that its chief effect is paralysis of voluntary muscles.

ABOVE FROM LEFT TO RIGHT: The mottled stem of Hemlock, *Conium maculatum*; Leaf of Hemlock; Leaf of Sweet Cicely, *Myrrhis odorata*.

It was also used for mania and epilepsy. Its action is similar to curare so it causes death by asphyxia. Lindley's comment (1838) was: 'a powerful narcotico-acrid plant, occasioning stupor, delirium, palsy and asphyxia … death in the most dreadful convulsions' and 'Stated by Aretaeus to be anti-aphrodisiac, [and] by Stoerck and Bergius to be the reverse'.

Hemlock closely resembles Cow Parsley (*Anthriscus sylvestris*), apart from having broader leaves and the mottled stem, as well as Wild Celery (*Apium graveolens*), and Sweet Cicely (*Myrrhis odorata*), which has resulted in poisoning and death when Hemlock has mistakenly been used in salads and sandwiches. As it grows freely on verges and in hedgerows it is always a risk for farmers and livestock.

Dioscorides wrote that the dried sap, applied topically, is good for shingles and erysipelas, stops nocturnal seminal emissions, relaxes genitalia, dries up milk, keeps young breasts small and make boys' testicles wither.

In many older herbals and pharmacopoeias *Conium maculatum*

was described either as being too toxic to use or the sap was carefully applied externally to treat shingles, inflammation, ulcers and gout. It is said that in the late medieval period of Arabic medicine a dampened 'anaesthetic sponge' containing hemlock, opium, henbane and sometimes aconitine was held over the nose of a patient, making painless surgical operations possible.

# ATROPA BELLADONNA

***Atropa belladonna*** L. Solanaceae. Deadly nightshade, *Solano furioso*, *Solanum somniferum* and *Solanum lethale*. Distribution: Europe.

It is so well known that this plant was the source of atropine, used for millennia, that we will use our space here to reveal the real origins of its name and debunk the myth that the name refers to beautiful ladies with dilated pupils because 'bella donna' is Italian for 'beautiful lady'. In short, it is

OPPOSITE: Hemlock, *Conium maculatum*, in the Socratic Garden

Hemlock was used by the Greeks and Romans to execute prisoners, most notably Socrates, as related in Plato's Phaedo. It was mixed with opium and taken with wine to ensure a speedier and less troublesome death.

named for the bringer of death and for the Bellonaria, priestesses of Bellona the goddess of war, and for their uses of it as 'war+gifts' – *bella+dona*.

The etymology of the genus, *Atropa*, is uncontroversial. It stems from Atropos, the oldest of the three Fates of Greek mythology who cut the thread of Life. Atropine is used to paralyse the autonomic nervous system by blocking acetylcholine receptors, thus stopping salivation, sweating, pupillary reflexes and other functions. The old names *S. furiosa, somniferum* and *lethale* mean *furious*, *sleep bringing* and *lethal*, reflecting its true etymology and its effect on the central nervous system properties in larger doses.

This northern European plant appears unknown to Theophrastus (in the original Greek, his plant is *Mandragora*), Dioscorides, Pliny and Ruel (1537, 1543). Under other names – e.g. *Solanum* – it appears in Fuchs (1542), Dodoens (1554), Lobel (1576), L'Escluse (1577) and Lyte (1578), who describe how it causes delirium and death. Nowhere can one find the idea that this poisonous plant was so-called because Italian society ladies put the juice of the berries into their eyes to give themselves large, doe-eyed and sexy pupils. Anyone who has had their pupils dilated for an ophthalmological examination will recollect the unpleasantness of being dazzled by sunlight and becoming excessively short-sighted as a result. Atropine will paralyse the pupil for about a week and if an Italian beauty ever did this, she would not have done it twice.

> **Named for the bringer of death and for the Bellonaria, priestesses of Bellona the goddess of war, and for their uses of it as 'war+gifts' – bella+dona.**

The earliest printed use of the name as '*Bella donna*' (sic – as two words), is in Matthiolus' commentary on Dioscorides (1558, but it may be in earlier editions). Dioscorides did not describe a plant which matches *A. belladonna* but Matthiolus adds an extra plant: *Solano maiora 'quae vulgo Bella donna vocatur'* (*Solanum major,* which is commonly called *Bella donna*) with an accompanying woodcut of *A. belladonna* and a description of its purple flowers and black berries. He describes how ingestion of the berries makes one mad, furious, maniacal and possessed, and can be fatal. He recommends a poultice of crushed leaves to soothe inflamed eyelids ('*Contusa folia oculorum, palpebrarumque phlegmonas leniunt*') but has nothing to indicate that it was used as a cosmetic, dilated the pupils or interfered with vision.

Its use as a cosmetic is suggested by Parkinson (1640) who writes:

> [*Solanum lethale*, Dwale or Deadly Nightshade] *is generally by the Italians called* Bella Donna, *either per Antiphrasin* [in a contrary sense to its normal meaning]*, because it is blacke, or as the Moores do account the fairest, that have the finest blacke skinne, or, as some have reported, because the Italian Dames, use the juice or distilled water thereof for a fucus* [a deceit or cosmetic]*, per adventure by the excessive cold quality, to take away their high colour and make them looke paler.*

As the juice is dark purple, it would be like a 'blusher' to give colour to the cheeks.

If anyone should know if *belladonna* was used for dilating pupils, it should be Linnaeus, who so named it in his *Species Plantarum* (1753). In his *Materia Medica* (1782) he gives its uses and notes its toxic, hallucinatory qualities, but makes no mention of dilating pupils. Examination of seventeen herbals and pharmacopoeias between 1542 and 1788, which call it *Belladonna,* shows no record of this either. Exceptions are Murray (1776), Professor of Medicine and Botany in the University of Göttingen, and Bergius (1782), Professor of Botany in Stockholm, who reported that it caused fixed dilated pupils. Bergius also notes that it caused a dry mouth and temporary blindness – presumably referring to the difficulty in seeing when dazzled by the sun. Dr Reimarus, in Germany in 1797, reported that pupil dilatation with *belladonna* was an aid to cataract surgery; thereafter its action is regularly reported in pharmacopoeias.[61] Paradoxically, it was noted that people with cataracts could see better with such dilated pupils as the pupil opened wide enough for light to come in round the edges of a central cataract.

The earliest reference for the name *belladonna* being derived from its use by ladies to dilate their pupils appears to be in Edward Ruddock's (1867) *The Homeopathic vade mecum of modern medicine and surgery* where he writes:

> *The plant derives … its specific name,* **Belladonna,** *from the Italian language, signifying a beautiful lady. This has been said to be owing to its being used as a cosmetic for the face; but more probably from it being employed to dilate the pupils – a practice still employed by some Parisian women, as it is supposed to confirm on them additional charms.*

This is at least 300 years too late.

ABOVE: Flower and berry of Deadly Nightshade. *Atropa belladonna*

It appears as *Belladona Italorum* in Pena & Lobel (1570); *Bella dona* in Dodoens (1583). Scaliger's Theophrastus[62] of 1644 illustrates it as *Belladona*. Gerard (1597, 1633) and Lewis (1761) also call it *bella dona* (all with one 'n') – Latin for 'wars' and 'gifts' (both are neuter nouns: *bellum,* plural *bella*; *donum,* plural *dona*). This reveals the correct etymology, which is supported by Scaliger who says *'Belladonna nomen est corruptum, ex bellonaria, quomodo solanum somniferum vocari scribit Apuleius'* (The name *Belladonna* is a corruption of Bellonaria, which was what Apuleius wrote that *Solanum somniferum* should be called).[3]

Lewis and Short's Latin dictionary translates: bellōnārĭa, ae, f., I. *the plant* Solanum, *used by the priests at the festival of Bellona* (v. Bellona), *App*[uleius]. *Herb*[arum]. *74.*[37]

Apuleius's *De Medicaminibus herbarum* (1537), chapter 74, notes several Solanaceae including *Bellonaria* (which Scaliger[62] says is *belladonna*): *'Bellonaria dicta est quod in bello ad cupides tingendas & inficiendas illa uterentur'* (It is called Bellonaria because in war it is used to stain and poison spear heads). The Bellonaria were the *berserker* priestesses of Bellona, the goddess of war (sister to Mars). It makes a more credible story that the poisonous *Atropa belladonna* was *bella dona*, for making spears more deadly and, if ingested, a drug to make the priestesses furious fighters; a useful 'gift' for making 'war'. Nothing to do with dilated pupils, even if the Bellonaria were female and when stoned would have had such pupils.

Finally, if the author(s) of the name, writing in Latin, wished it to mean 'beautiful lady' it would have been called *'bella domina'*, for *donna* is not found in Latin.

# ORIGANUM DICTAMNUS

**Origanum dictamnus** L. Lamiaceae. Dittany of Crete, Hop marjoram. Distribution: Crete.

his tiny, prostrate, herbaceous plant with its furry leaves and pale mauve flowers is a delight to behold, but its role in a 3500-year-old story told in Virgil's *Aeneid* makes it interesting as well. Virgil recounts how the goddess Venus/Aphrodite used this plant to wash her son Aeneas' deadly arrow wound during the Trojan wars of circa 1200BCE: the arrow promptly falls out and Dittany became one of the oldest documented medicinal plants in European history.

Culpeper summarises its uses from his wide reading of classical authors, calling it:

*Dictamny, or Dittany of Creet, … brings away dead children, hastens women's travail* [labour]*, brings away the afterbirth, the very smell of it drives away venemous beasts, so deadly an enemy is it to poison, it's an admirable remedy against wounds and Gunshot; wounds made with poisoned weapons, draws out splinters, broken bones etc. They say the goats and deer in Creet* [Crete]*, being wounded with arrows, eat this herb, which makes the arrows fall out of themselves.*

## 'For taketh never so little of the right Dictamnus into the mouth it setteth it presently on a fire'

Dioscorides, Pliny and Theophrastus all have this information. Pliny writes at length about its powers to induce labour and to expel a dead foetus, including when there is a transverse lie: 'Dictamnus … hath no peer … it sendeth out the dead child, yea though it lay overthwart and stuck crosse in the birth.' So powerful was its property that Pliny claimed that pregnant women would go into labour even if the plant was in the same room or they just smelt its fragrance. He describes how to identify it by its taste '… at the tongues end it is hot and biting … for taketh never so little of the right Dictamnus into the mouth it setteth it presently on a fire'. We have never plucked up the courage to try this.

TOP: *Origanum dictamnus*, Dittany of Crete
ABOVE: Flower of *Origanum dictamnus*

ASPICIT ET INSPICIT

# PHYTOGNOMONICA
## IO. BAPTISTAE
## PORTAE NEAP.

*OCTO LIBRIS CONTENTA.*

IN QVIBVS NOVA, FACILLIMAQVE
affertur methodus, qua plantarum, anima-
lium, metallorū, rerum deniq; omniū
ex prima extimæ faciei inspectio-
ne quiuis abditas vires
assequatur?

ACCEDVNT AD HAEC CONFIR-
manda infinita propemodū selectiora secre-
ta, summo labore, temporis dispendio,
& impensarum iactura vesti-
gata, explorataq;.

CVM PRIVILEGIO.

NEAPOLI, Apud Horatium Saluianum. 1588.

# PLANTS ILLUSTRATING THE DOCTRINES OF SIGNATURES AND HUMOURS

These two doctrines help us to understand why our medical predecessors picked certain plants to be used as medicines. However, therapeutic properties were claimed for many plants without recourse to either doctrine or to the astrological hypotheses of Nicholas Culpeper (1616–54). In particular, plants which were poisonous, or acted on the nervous system, were identified by simple observation.

The Doctrine of Signatures may be based on a belief that the Creator made all plants for mankind's use and indicated by their shape, colour, etc., what illness they treated. Additionally, if an illness occurred in a certain area or country, then the Creator would put the plant that cured it nearby. While Theophrastus refers to this belief, it is Dodoens (1583) who must be given credit for first using the term *'Doctrino vero de signaturis stirpium'* [The true doctrine of the signature of plants]. Porta (1588) wrote a whole book on it with explanatory woodcuts. The followers of Paracelsus (1493–1541) supported it. Coles (1657) may be regarded as the first English exponent of the concept, although he never used the phrase, but thereafter it disappears from published European works. It never had much practical application. The belief that all species were divinely created at the beginning of the world and were immutable persisted until Charles Darwin's *On the Origin of Species* (1859).

TOP: Bust of Hippocrates, who conceived the Doctrine of the Humours
ABOVE: Giovanni Baptista Porta
OPPOSITE: Title page of Porta's *Phytognomica* (1588), which propounded the Doctrine of Signatures

**The Doctrine of the Humours is based on the belief that the body is constructed of four 'humours' of black bile, blood (hot), yellow bile and phlegm (cold).**

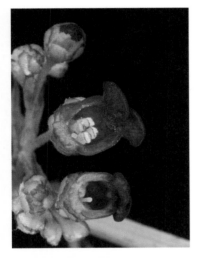

ABOVE: The haemorrhoid-resembling flowers of Figwort (Pilewort) *Scrophularia nodosa* and its nodular roots that resemble tuberculous lymph nodes (scrofula)

The Doctrine of the Humours is based on the belief that the body is constructed of four 'humours' of black bile, blood (hot), yellow bile and phlegm (cold). These correspond to the four 'elements' that make up the world; earth, air, fire and water, which were propounded by Empedocles (490 – ca. 430BCE). The forces of attraction, Eros (love), and rejection, Eris (strife), regulated their properties and interactions. Any imbalance of the humours caused an illness, especially of the hot and cold humours, a *distemper* or a *dyscrasia*. An illness due to a perceived excess of one humour could be cured by plants with an excess of the opposite element. An excess of the cold, phlegmatic element – a 'cold' – could be treated with hot red wine with spices – mulled wine. The converse was also practised and as late as the early twentieth century William Osler, the doyen of the medical profession, was still recommending blood-letting for treating fevers such as pneumonia, perceived as an excess of the hot element.

# SCROPHULARIA NODOSA

***Scrophularia nodosa*** L. Scrophulariaceae. Figwort. Distribution: Europe.

ig is a medieval word for piles (haemorrhoids) and a 'wort' is a plant, so 'figwort' means 'pile plant' – a plant which treats piles. The flowers, which present an open orifice with two dark red lobular protrusions, need little imagination to see how the name has arisen. Linnaeus gave it its Latin name in 1753 and added 'nodosa' which refers to the nodular roots which resemble the swollen lymph nodes of the King's Evil, or scrofula. This was the name for a tuberculous infection of the lymph nodes in the neck, which was supposed to be cured by the touch of a King. George I abolished the practice in Britain. The College has a copy of a Proclamation of Charles II concerning the ceremony of touching for

*Hepatica nobilis.* The three-lobed leaves indicated its use in hepatic disorders as the liver has three lobes

the King's Evil in Whitehall on 9 January 1683. Needless to say, figwort/*Scrophularia* is ineffective in the treatment of either condition. It does contain cardiac glycosides, similar to foxglove and equally toxic, but has never been used for heart failure.

# HEPATICA NOBILIS

**Hepatica nobilis** Mill. Ranunculaceae. Liverwort – not to be confused with the Bryophytes with the same name. Distribution: North America, but now a common garden plant.

his plant has three-lobed leaves, like the liver, so was used for treating hepatic disorders and called *Hepatica*. It is little used in modern herbalism but was formerly employed in treating disorders of the liver and gall bladder, indigestion and so on, but it is highly toxic. The related species, *Hepatica acutiloba*, was widely used for liver disorders in the 1880s, with up to 200,000 kilos of leaves being harvested per annum to make liver tonics. This was discontinued when it was found they caused jaundice. Gerard (1633) calls it *Hepaticum trifolium*, Noble Liverwort, Golden Trefoile and herbe Trinity and writes: 'It is reported to be good against weakness of the liver which proceedeth from a hot cause, for it cooleth and strengtheneth it not a little'. Quincy (1718) writes 'and some are fond of it because of the resemblance it bears of the liver and spleen in its leaves, but that Signature Philosophy is exploded. Not much used …'. It did have an affinity to liver disorders, but caused them rather than cured.

TOP: Woodcut of *Pulmonaria officinalis* from Lyte's Herbal (1578)
BELOW: *Pulmonaria officinalis*

# PULMONARIA OFFICINALIS

***Pulmonaria officinalis*** L. Boraginaceae.
*Pulmonaria* or Lungwort. Distribution: Europe.

oth common names are applied to a lichen, *Lobaria pulmonaria,* and a perennial plant in the Boraginaceae, *Pulmonaria officinalis*. This is the latter. Lyte (1578) has a woodcut of our plant and also calls it Sage of Jerusalem and says it is of 'no particular use in physicke, but is much used in meates and salads with eggs, as is also Cowslippes and Primroses, whereunto in temperature it is much alike.' He lists and describes the lichen separately. Culpeper said he found many sorts of *lunguewort* and that they 'helpe infirmities of the lungues, as hoarseness, coughs, wheezing, shortnesse of breath etc.' Coles (1657) who espouses the Doctrine of

Signatures in a way unrivalled by any other English author, might have been expected to confirm the concept that the mottled leaves looked like the cut surface of a lung, which indicates their purpose, but he only mentions the lichen. However, Porta's beautiful book on the Doctrine, *Phytognomica* (1588), is clear that the plant called *Pulmonaria* has hairy leaves like a bugloss, spotted white with purple flowers, commonly called '*cynoglossa*' (with a woodcut which could be *Pulmonaria officinalis*) which indicate its use for ulcerated lungs, spitting blood, shortness of breath and asthma. The roots are also thought to be good against 'ulcers of the lungs'. Quincy (1718) writes: '… it has a glutinous juice … and heals ulcers and erosions. It is commended in coughs and spitting of blood but is little used either in the Shop or Prescriptions'. Woodville (1790) writes that it has no medicinal effect, but Linnaeus (1753) kept its medicinal, historical name when he gave it the name which we still use today.

It is not used in modern medicine. It is in the family Boraginaceae whose species are often rich in pyrrolizidine alkaloids that cause liver toxicity and cancers, although the levels in *Pulmonaria officinalis* may not be toxic. Whatever our ancestors believed, it has no therapeutic effects in lung disorders.

# ACONITUM SPECIES

***Aconitum lycoctonum*** L. Ranunculaceae. Leopard's Bane. Distribution: Europe and Asia, but now a common garden plant. We grow the subspecies *neopolitanum* and *vulparia*.

***Aconitum napellus*** L. Ranunculaceae. Wolf's Bane, Monk's Hood. Distribution: Europe.

***Aconitum carmichaelii***. Debeaux. Ranunculaceae. Sichuan Aconite. Distribution: China.

heophrastus (371–287BCE) has two of the earliest examples of plants whose shapes were associated with function, although they did not indicate their main actions and uses. He writes:

*Some roots are of peculiar shape, as that of the plant called 'scorpion-plant'* [Ed. Leopard's Bane – *Aconitum lycoctonum*] *and that of polypody* [*Polypodium cambricum* a close relative of *P. glycyrrhiza*]. *For the former is like a scorpion and is also useful against the sting of that creature and for certain other purposes. The root of polypody is rough and has suckers like the tentacles of the polyp* [octopus] *… and, if one wears it as an amulet, they say that one does not get a polypus. It has a leaf like the great fern, and it grows on rocks.*

He goes on to write about *Aconitum napellus*, Wolf's Bane, and describes how poisonous it is, stating (incorrectly) that it kills painlessly and that there is no antidote, but: '… useless to those who do not understand it; in fact it is said that it is not lawful even to have it in one's possession, under pain of death'.

Plants of *Aconitum* are available from almost every garden centre and, while perfectly legal, they contain aconitine, a highly poisonous alkaloid. This, however, is extremely bitter and so difficult to use as a poison. The sap of *A. carmichaelii* was used in China as an arrow poison and its equally poisonous European counterpart, *A. napellus*, was used to kill wolves and dogs. Lindley (1838) describes how three out of five people who drank alcohol to which had been added the leaves of *A. napellus*, having mistaken it for Lovage (*Levisticum officinale*), died within three hours of 'vomiting, purging, burning in the throat, colic and swelling in the belly'. Nevertheless, up to the twentieth century, physicians used the leaves for almost everything, including 'paralysis, epilepsy, rheumatic and neuralgic pains, dropsy, uterine complaints, intermittent fevers, etc, etc'. Fortunately for the patients they used tiny doses. Aconitine causes respiratory paralysis, bradycardia (slowing of the pulse), cardiac arrhythmias, tingling, sweating, gastric cramps, diarrhoea and death, either by ingestion or by absorption through the mucous membranes and the skin.[92] It is advisable to wear thick gloves when handling the plant. There is no antidote, but atropine (from *Atropa belladonna* – Deadly Nightshade) reverses the bradycardia and may be lifesaving. The belief that one poison was an antidote to another was a tenet of the Doctrine of Signatures, and while acting on this was usually fatal, chance occasionally makes it true.

**The notorious 'curry murder', as it was dubbed by the London *Evening Standard*, happened in 2009 when Lakhvir Kaur Singh added *Aconitum ferox* juice to the curry being eaten by her ex-lover and his new, younger, fiancée.**

The notorious 'curry murder', as it was dubbed by the London *Evening Standard*, happened in 2009 when Lakhvir Kaur Singh added *Aconitum ferox* juice to the curry being eaten by her ex-lover and his new, younger, fiancée. The man died within hours, the girl survived. Under the headline 'Mansion gardener killed by poison plant', *The Times* in 2014 reported on a gardener who died of multiple organ failure five days after being admitted to hospital. The cause was tentatively attributed to the sap of *Aconitum* being absorbed through the skin while handling it in the garden where he worked. Despite its toxicity, it is still widely used in Chinese herbal medicine and has caused poisoning, but in the UK its use is restricted and it can only be dispensed by a herbal practitioner for external use following a one-to-one consultation, or by prescription from a registered doctor or dentist. There are plenty of wild and garden plants which are almost as toxic: if one wanted a truly 'safe' garden, one would have to stick to grasses.

OPPOSITE TOP: *Aconitum lycoctonum*, Leopard's Bane LEFT: *Aconitum carmichaelii*, Sichuan aconite RIGHT: *Aconitum napellus*, Wolf's Bane, Monk's Hood

*Polypodium glycyrrhiza*. The rhizomes of the related *P. cambrica* were believed to cure nasal polyps

# POLYPODIUM GLYCYRRHIZA

**Polypodium glycyrrhiza** D.C.Eaton. Polypodiaceae. Licorice fern. Distribution: Russia, North America.

 heophrastus's second plant is a fern, probably *Polypodium cambricum*, a lithophyte from Greece, which is very similar to *P. glycyrrhiza*, which we grow in the North American bed. 'Polypody' means 'many feet', referring to the branching, nobbly rhizomes which resemble octopus tentacles, so were used for treating nasal polyps (Parkinson, 1640). The polypody of the *Pharmacopoeia Londinensis* (1618) and Culpeper (1649) was *P. vulgare*.

# CAPSICUM ANNUUM

**Capsicum annuum** L. Solanaceae. Chilli pepper and Salad pepper. Distribution: Central and South America.

 'hot plant' in the concept of the Doctrine of the Humours. It originated from Mexico (although the centre of *Capsicum* evolution was much earlier in Bolivia) and includes the bland salad peppers and the hot chilli peppers, of which capsaicin (sometimes called capsicain), from the lining of the inside of the chilli, is the main active ingredient. Chilli comes from the Aztec language of the Nahuatl people. It was reputedly introduced to Europe by Columbus at the end of the fifteenth century. It had been cultivated in Mexico since 4000BCE and used in cooking since 7200BCE.

After its introduction to Europe, its cultivation very rapidly became worldwide. It appears as a description by Bock (1539) with the name *teutschem Pfeffer* [Indian pepper]. The first illustration as *Siliquastrum* (Latin for a herb with a sharp biting taste) was published by Fuchs (1542), who did not realise it came from the Americas as he mis-identified it as the *Siliquastrum* described by Pliny, Dioscorides and Avicenna. Lyte (1578) notes its humoural value as being 'hot and drie in the third degree'. He recommended it for dressing meat and noted that it 'warmeth the stomach' and was good for a sore throat, scrofula and topically got rid of spots. Lindley (1838) wrote:

*It is employed in medicine, in combination with* Cinchona *in intermittent and lethargic affections, and also in atonic gout, dyspepsia accompanied by flatulence, tympanitis, paralysis etc. Its most valuable application appears however to be in* cynanche maligna [=severe sore throat, with impending suffocation] *and* scarlatina maligna [=severe scarlet fever], *used either as a gargle or administered internally.*

> **Gargling with chilli sauce when afflicted by a sore throat does not bear thinking about. Its present use medically has been for inhibiting an overactive bladder and for pain relief.**

Gargling with chilli sauce when afflicted by a sore throat does not bear thinking about. Its present use medically has been for inhibiting an overactive bladder and for pain relief, applied locally for pain from muscle injury, to post-herpetic neuralgia. Capsaicin acts on pain and heat-sensing nerve endings triggering the sensation of pain. Repeated exposure to capsaicin depletes the neurotransmitter substance P that carries the pain message and may even cause reversible degeneration of the nerve endings, preventing the sensation of pain/heat from any cause. It is a banned substance in equestrian events at the Olympics because of its analgesic effects. At the other extreme, capsaicin is the active ingredient in 'pepper' aerosol defence sprays. Capsaicin has been shown, experimentally, to kill cancer cells by attacking their mitochondria; particular interest has concentrated on its ability to reduce the size of tumours of the pancreas and prostate. An additional use for *Capsicum* was as the principal source for the manufacture of vitamin C in the mid-twentieth century.

Various cultivars are used in cooking and the strength (i.e. how hot they are) is measured in Scoville units. A standard chilli pepper used in England would be around 5000 Scovilles; the hottest peppers are rated at over one million Scoville units.

If invited by a 'friend' to eat a small, dangerous-looking chilli, always acquiesce and bite off the very tip, make the appropriate 'aaagh' noises and follow this with 'Not bad, now you try it'. Capsaicin is not present in the tip of a chilli, only in the lining of the seed chamber, as your 'friend' will discover if he/she takes up the challenge.

FOLLOWING SPREAD LEFT: *Capsicum annuum* as *Siliquastrum*, annotated 'Ginny pepper/Indian pepper' from Christian Egenolph (1562) RIGHT: Fruit of *Capsicum annuum*

# PLANTS WITH AN ASSOCIATION WITH THE COLLEGE

Here we have *Fothergilla gardenii*, named after John Fothergill, a Licentiate who never became a Fellow because he was not an Anglican; and *Punica granatum*, the pomegranate which came onto the Coat of Arms granted to us in 1546 by King Henry VIII.

## FOTHERGILLA GARDENII

**Fothergilla gardenii** L. Hamamelidaceae. Distribution: North America.

 genus in the witch hazel family named by the great botanist, Linnaeus, to honour John Fothergill LRCP, FRS (1712–80), who sent him many North American plants.

Fothergill was a Quaker physician of great distinction who campaigned without success to abolish the religious bigotry of our College, which prevented non-conformists from being elected to the Fellowship. It is for this reason that *Fothergilla gardenii* has been selected to represent the eponymous physicians commemorated in the College Garden. The specific name *gardenii* is also of medical significance, being named after the Scottish physician Alexander Garden FRS (1730–91) of Charleston, South Carolina, with whom Fothergill corresponded and after whom *Gardenia* is named.

John Fothergill was an outstanding eighteenth-century physician, Quaker, philanthropist and plantsman. Fothergill lectured on mouth-to-mouth resuscitation at the Royal Society, published as *Observations on a case … of recovering a man dead in appearance by distending the lungs with air.* He published the first account of diphtheria, *An account of the sore throat attended with ulcers* in 1748 (later accounts were entitled *An account of the putrid sore throat*) and described trigeminal neuralgia, *Of a painful affection of the face.* He became extremely successful. During the epidemics of influenza in 1775 and 1776 he is

OPPOSITE: *Fothergilla gardenii*

John Fothergill (1712–80)

**His greenhouse extended for 80 metres and contained over 3000 species. Fothergill had the flowers painted and on his death the collection of around 2000 paintings was sold, ending up with the Empress of Russia.**

said to have had sixty patients daily. With an income of over £7000 a year he purchased a large estate at Upton. Fothergill spared no expense to obtain and cultivate exotic plants from all over the world for his garden, which was visited by international dignitaries and botanists. His greenhouse extended for 80 metres and contained over 3000 species. Fothergill had the flowers painted and on his death the collection of around 2000 paintings was sold, ending up with the Empress of Russia. These paintings have recently been identified in Russia and attempts are being made to get them back to the United Kingdom. Fothergill also amassed an outstanding collection of shells which he left to his fellow Licentiate, William Hunter, and which are now in the Hunterian Museum in Glasgow.

Fothergill never married; his sister Anne kept house for him until his death in 1780, aged sixty-nine, from 'suppression of urine'. At autopsy this was shown to be due to 'a schirrous enlargement of the prostate which compressed the neck of the bladder so as to prevent the introduction of a catheter' (Elliott, 1781).

## PUNICA GRANATUM

**Punica granatum** L. Lythraceae. Pomegranate, *Granatum malum*, *Malum punicum,* balustines. Distribution: Eastern Mediterranean to Himalayas. Planted in the Middle Eastern bed at the top of the College lawn in 1977 to celebrate the Silver Jubilee of HM Queen Elizabeth II.

 n the Royal College of Physicians' coat of arms, granted to the College by Henry VIII in 1546, there is a rather indistinct blob of fruit, originally described as a 'powme granate golde', a golden pomegranate. The book on the College and its collections (McDonald, & Moss-Gibbons, 2001) states that it is there because it 'cured burning agues [fevers]'. The suggestion that it was taken from the coat of arms of Catherine of Aragon, who married Henry VIII in 1509 (divorced 1533,

died 1536), is an unlikely alternative, as Dr Stuart Mason, former editor of the *Journal of the RCP,* has noted.[45] It does not even look like the one on our coat of arms, which appears to be taken from the woodcut captioned *Malum punicum* in Jean Ruel's (1543) commentaries on Dioscorides, which we believe to be the earliest known printed image. The picture fits; the date fits.

If a treatment for fevers was the reason, then one would expect the medical texts of the period around 1545 to reflect the then prevalent humoral theory of medicine and to state that cooling, cold, refreshing pomegranate juice was an antidote to the excess of the hot humours which 'caused' a fever. Gilbertus Anglicus (1510) is one of the few that do, writing about: '… acid pomegranates, whose juice cools the stomach and relieves thirst', albeit regarding food fit for travellers.

Dioscorides wrote that the sweet, juicy pomegranate creates a 'degree of warmth in the stomach … consequently it is unsuitable for people running a fever'. Ruel cautions against using it in fevers (1543).

Dodoens (1554) agreed with Gilbertus Anglicus that sour pomegranates were good for fevers and this is repeated by Henry Lyte (1578):

> *Pomegranates be colde and somewhat astringent … it is very good against al hoate agues* [fevers] *… especially the iuce of the sower pomegranates … for the sweete pomegranates (because they engender a little heate and breede winde) are not very meete to be used in agues.*

The argument about its use in fevers continued until 1707 when Hans Sloane, President of the RCP, wrote of pomegranates: 'The Fruit is cooling, good in Fevers, quenching Thirst, drying and binding, and withal very stomachic'.

Of its other properties, Culpeper makes no mention of the fruit, but says of the flowers '… they stop fluxes [diarrhoea] and the Terms [periods] in women'. Gerard (1633) says that the cravings of pregnant women can be abolished with the juice, and perhaps it was scurvy which was being treated effectively when he reports that the juice was very effective against spitting of blood and for loose teeth.

A tincture of the bark was used as a vermifuge (for killing intestinal worms), with the secondary use that it doubled as a permanent ink which did not fade in sunlight. This was very useful if one wanted to write a letter to thank one's physician for his treatment. It is reported to be effective against fevers, as a diuretic, to lower blood sugar and to be both antibacterial and antiviral (van Wyk, 2000). In the 'muthi' medicine tradition of South Africa the fruit rind is still used for diarrhoea and stomach ache and the bark as a vermifuge, but undesirable side effects make this dangerous. Pomegranate bark can only be sold by registered pharmacies in the UK, but pomegranate juice has gained a reputation as a 'superfood', a mythical concept of today's mass media.

TOP: Flowers and fruit of the pomegranate, *Punica granatum*. BELOW LEFT: Woodcut of a pomegranate from Jean Ruel's commentaries on Dioscorides (1543) RIGHT: Pomegranate on the College coat of arms

# PLANTS FROM THE COLLEGE'S PHARMACOPOEIA LONDINENSIS (1618)

Here are the plants which we highlight to commemorate what is, arguably, the most important task that the College ever undertook – the publication of a London pharmacopoeia to standardise the contents of compound medicines, a book which continues now as the *British Pharmacopoeia*. In August 1617, the Apothecaries parted company from the Grocers and set up on their own. In response the College issued the *Pharmacopoea Londinensis* (sic) in May 1618. This was a legally binding text which listed all the medicines that physicians could prescribe, and apothecaries could dispense, and how to make them.

The College had been discussing the preparation of a London pharmacopoeia since 1585, but the book produced by the printer, Edward Griffin, and the publisher, John Marriott, was merely a cut down version of the *Pharmacopoeia Augustana* of 1613 (Minderer, 1613). This in turn was a modification of the first *Augustana* (Occo III, 1564), which was based on the *Dispensatorium* of Valerius Cordus (1546). The 1613 edition had additions from the novel chemical therapies of Paracelsus and these have carried across into the College's pharmacopoeia. While Paracelsian ideas were not accepted by all, Theodore de Mayerne and Thomas Moffat, two of the College's pharmacopoeia committee, were supporters of them. The College's pharmacopoeia used the

ABOVE: Title page of the first edition of the *Pharmacopoe[i]a Londinensis*, 1618
OPPOSITE: Jane Knowles, Head Gardener to the College since 2005, working in the beds of the *Pharmacopoeia Londinensis*

**The publication of *Pharmacopoeia* in May 1618 caused a frisson in the College and this, the first edition, was hastily withdrawn.**

same font, the same layout of the columns, indents and margins, almost the same wording and in the same order, as the *Augustana* of 1613. It looks as if the College gave Marriot a redacted copy (the *Augustana* was overly long, with 1306 medicines) and said 'copy that'. The text was in Latin and the uses of the medicines as given in the *Augustana* were omitted, for the physicians had no wish for the apothecaries to learn how to treat patients: that was the prerogative of the College's physicians.

The publication of the *Pharmacopoeia* in May 1618 caused a frisson in the College and this, the first edition, was hastily withdrawn. A revised edition was issued in December the same year. The College blamed the printer for undue haste and printing errors, but it is possible that credit for some compound medications devised by its Fellows had not been given, so noses were out of joint. Whatever the real reason, everything in the May edition remained in the December issue. Urdang (1944) counted 680 simples (1190 in December) and 712 compound medicines (963 in December) which implies that some of the College physicians wanted their favourite

Plants whose flowers were used to make medicines in the College's *Pharmacopoeia Londinensis* of 1618

medicines included. In particular, there were three times as many animal parts listed as ingredients and 50% more minerals, which suggested that the Paracelsians (who favoured such things) were becoming prominent in the College. It became the standard pharmacopoeia and the contents were protected by a copyright granted to John Marriott by James I for twenty-one years, with a penalty of £5 per book for any copies, importations or translations.

Thirty-one years after first publication the great herbalist, Nicholas Culpeper, translated the December edition of the *Pharmacopoeia Londinensis* into English, as *A Physical Directory* (1649) and added information on the uses of all the medicines and the simples, mostly abstracted from earlier writers and the *Augustana*. For three old pence anyone could buy a copy and treat their illnesses with the simples, most of which were easily available in the countryside.

Jane Knowles, Head Gardener to the College, researched, designed and planted the eight beds in the precinct, setting out the plants according to whether the flowers, the roots, the seeds, etc., were used. Few are now used to make modern medicines, but our progress in pharmacy and therapeutics can be dated from these early beginnings, the start of clear documentation in this country. Many of these medicines had uses that dated back to the first century of the Christian Era but, as would be expected, disappeared from mainstream use in the twentieth century, while continuing as traditional herbal remedies – albeit often with non-traditional uses.

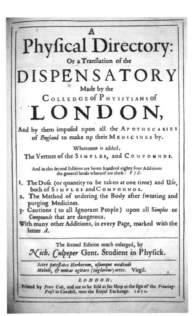

TOP: Title page of Culpeper's translation of the College's *Pharmacopoeia Londinensis* (1649)
ABOVE: Portrait of Nicholas Culpeper, 1650

*Borago officinalis.* Borage with blue flowers

**This is a plant whose uses remained unchanged for two thousand years until someone in the twentieth century noticed it could cause cirrhosis and death from liver failure.**

# BORAGO OFFICINALIS

**Borago officinalis** L. Boraginaceae. Borage. Distribution: Europe. It is called 'Borago' in the College's *Pharmacopoeia*. The flowers and the leaves were used.

orago's specific name, *officinalis*, indicates it was used in the 'offices' – the consulting clinics – of medieval monks. Linnaeus kept this ancient name when he systematised plant nomenclature in 1753. It has a wonderfully hairy leaf and flowers with the most exotic blue of any on the planet. This is a plant whose uses remained unchanged for two thousand years until someone in the twentieth century noticed it could cause cirrhosis and death from liver failure. Pliny says: 'This herb hath one special property above the rest, that if it be put into a cup of wine, it cheereth the heart and maketh them that drink it pleasant and merry' – a very good reason for it to be added to Pimm's. Culpeper echoes Pliny: '... comforts the heart, cheers the spirit, drives away sadness and melancholy', but adds 'they are rather laxative than binding; help swooning and heart qualms, breed special good blood; help consumptions, madness and such as are much weakened by sickness' and the flowers 'strengthen the heart and brain, and are profitable in fevers'. Lindley (1838), while noting its cucumber flavour and that it was added to cordials, doubted that it had any 'exhilarating qualities'. He wrote that it 'was once esteemed as a pectoral medicine [i.e. for chest complaints].' It has the potential to be hepatotoxic when ingested, because it contains pyrrolizidines, and is genotoxic and carcinogenic, so the UK Medicines and Healthcare Products Regulatory Agency (MHRA) advises that it should not be taken internally.[80]

*Calendula officinalis*

# CALENDULA OFFICINALIS

***Calendula officinalis*** L. Asteraceae. Pot marigold, common marigold, ruds or ruddles. Distribution: Europe. It is called 'Calendula' in the College's *Pharmacopoeia*. The flowers and the leaves were used.

 *alendula* was so called because it was said to flower most commonly at the first of each month – the 'calends' (Coles, 1657). The Doctrine of Signatures indicated that as the flowers resembled the pupil of the eye (along with *Arnica, Inula* and the ox-eye daisy), it was good for eye disorders (Porta, 1588). Coles writes '… the distilled water … helpeth red and watery eyes, being washed therewith, which it does by Signature'. Culpeper says that the leaves '… loosen the belly, the juice held in the mouth helps the toothache and takes away any inflammation, or hot swelling being bathed with it mixed with a little vinegar'. John Lindley (1838) wrote that the petals were 'formerly much employed as a carminative [a drug for treating flatus]; it is chiefly used now to adulterate saffron'. The UK MHRA warns that it should be avoided in pregnancy as it is a uterine stimulant.[80] Flowers are added to salads and stews (although it is never suggested that one eats more than one). The plant contains carotenoids, flavoxanthin, auroxanthin, lutein, beta-carotene, saponins, sesquiterpene glucosides and triterpenes. Turner (1551) writes that the flowers were used by ladies 'to make their hair yellow' and: 'a perfume made of the dry flowers of this herb, and put to the convenient place, bring down the secondes [placenta, afterbirth]'. Currently, it is used to make hand creams and food dyes. Skin sensitivity may occur. It is no longer licensed for internal use.

# MELILOTUS OFFICINALIS

**Melilotus officinalis** Lam. Papilionaceae. Meliot, Yellow Sweet Clover. Distribution: Europe to East Asia but following introduction to North America it has become widely distributed there. It is called 'Meliloti' in the College's *Pharmacopoeia*.

opular beliefs that traditional herbal uses of a plant will be an indication of its medical usefulness are widely held. As almost every European plant had a 'herbal' use at one time, it would not be surprising if this was sometimes true. However this 'doctrine' has no more validity than the Doctrines of Signatures and the Humours. Meliot is a good example, for its 2000-year-old herbal uses bear no relationship to its current medicinal use. Culpeper wrote, merely paraphrasing Pliny and others before him:

*Meliotus. Meliot. Inwardly taken provokes urine, breaks the stone, clenseth the reins and bladder, cutteth and clenseth the lungs of tough phlegm; the juice dropped into the eyes cleers the sight, into the ears mitigates pain and noise there; the head bathed with the juice mixed with vinegar takes away the pains thereof, outwardly in poultices, it assuages swellings in the privities, and elsewhere.*

In current herbal medicine the dry leaves are applied to varicose veins and haemorrhoids.

The plant's actual medical value as a source of an anticoagulant also has no connection with its historic use. If the plant is wet when harvested it becomes mouldy, and fungal action converts one of its chemicals, dicoumarine, to dicoumarol, a vitamin K antagonist and so an anticoagulant. It causes internal bleeding in cattle that eat it. Warfarin was developed from it and is currently the most widely used anticoagulant in the treatment and prevention of blood clotting, thrombosis and embolism. None of these uses could be predicted from its herbal uses – and, of course, fresh Meliot has no anticoagulant activity. Overdoses of Warfarin can be treated with vitamin K, and high levels of this vitamin in certain green leaf vegetables and herbs (e.g. basil, kale and parsley) antagonise its anticoagulant effectiveness.

# ACORUS CALAMUS, ACORUS GRAMINEUS

**Acorus calamus** L. Acoraceae. Sweet flag, Sweet calamus, Myrtle flag, Calamus, Flagroot. Distribution: Asia, southeastern USA. It is called 'Calamus aromaticus' in the College's *Pharmacopoeia*.

ixteenth and seventeenth century herbalists had two plants called *Calamus* – *Calamus aromaticus* and *Calamus odoratus*. The plant simply known as *Acorus* in Rembert Dodoens' *Pemptades* of 1583 was neither of these. By 1640 Parkinson had given it a binomial as *Acorus verus* or

ABOVE LEFT TO RIGHT: *Melilotus officinalis*; *Acorus* from Dodoens' *Stirpium Historiae Pemptades Sex* (1583) is probably *Iris pseudoacorus* which was substituted for the unobtainable *Acorus calamus* in the sixteenth century; *Acorus gramineus* 'Oborozuki' showing the rhizome

*Calamus officinarum*, which is what we grow in the *Pharmacopoeia* beds, under the name *Acorus calamus* as given by Linnaeus in 1753.

Culpeper gives its standard uses for the seventeenth century: '... binds, strengthens, stops fluxes of the belly [diarrhoea], and immoderate flowing of the terms [heavy periods] in women, a drachm being taken in red wine every morning'.

Oil of calamus, made from the roots and rhizome, contains beta-asarone which is carcinogenic, nephrotoxic and causes convulsions.[80] Its former uses in aromatherapy and perfumes are now banned. It should not be taken internally and its use has been banned in most countries. Aqueous solutions are always safer and small amounts are permitted in the EU as a food flavouring – but not in the USA. In South African herbal medicine it is used to treat diarrhoea and the powdered root is used as toothpaste.

**Acorus gramineus**. Aiton. Acoraceae. Grassy leaved sweet flag. Distribution: Temperate and tropical Asia.

An important species in the same genus is *Acorus gramineus*, which is not listed in the College's *Pharmacopoeia*. It is used medicinally throughout Asia and the Philippines. It has the same multiplicity of uses as *A. calamus,* including treatment of arthritis, lumbago, muscle pains, indigestion, toothache, as a tonic, to increase the appetite, haemorrhage, treat intestinal ulceration, used as a sedative, for tinnitus, deafness, poor memory, unconsciousness during a fever, for treating insanity, as an insecticide, for abscesses and scabies and to protect young children from getting flatus when someone compliments them on their appearance – the condition known as 'usog'. It might be worth mentioning in a College membership examination (MRCP) *Viva* if the examiner's interest in passing you is flagging, or you are looking for questions for the Christmas quiz.

The work of William Withering ... made the purple foxglove, *Digitalis purpurea*, the most widely recognised medicinal plant.

# PLANTS THAT WERE MILESTONES IN THE DISCOVERY OF MEDICINES

Many milestones occurred in the progress of medicine, but the work of William Withering (1741–99), who by years of observation on his patients and the effects of the plant on their fluid retention, made purple foxglove, *Digitalis purpurea*, the most widely recognised medicinal plant.

While we do not grow *Cinchona*, tropical trees, in our Garden, as they would not survive the winter, its extensive presence in our Pharmaceutical Society herbarium attests to its importance over 500 years as the key which unlocked the treatment of malaria.

*Artemisia annua*, with an ancient history in Chinese medicine, sprang into importance during the Vietnam War, where malaria was killing as many people as the weapons of war. Even now, although of the two million people who contract malaria per week, up to 14,000 die, there would be many more fatalities (there were twice as many in 2002) but for Artemisinin and other drugs. The spin-off of other therapies from *Artemisia* is one of the most startling of all developments in modern therapeutics.

The yam, *Dioscorea*, which gave us the contraceptive pill and other steroids, changed society and medicine for ever. Pain management has always been an important aspect of the physician's task, so we have included the discovery of Lidocaine (lignocaine) from Barley, *Hordeum vulgare*, and the Giant Reed, *Arundo donax*, in our selection.

ABOVE: William Withering, who pioneered clinical observation of medical treatment
OPPOSITE: *Digitalis purpurea*

*Digitalis lanata*, the woolly foxglove from which digoxin is extracted

# DIGITALIS PURPUREA

*Digitalis purpurea* L. Plantaginaceae. Common foxglove, Purple foxglove. Distribution: North Africa, Europe.

ne of the Garden Fellows, walking far from civilisation in the province of Huanuco in the Peruvian Andes, found *Digitalis purpurea* growing in the cloud forest near a Quechua village. The fact it was an 'Excelsior' cultivar made one wonder how a seed packet had found its way to this distant backwater of the world, lacking roads, electricity, phones or books. Despite this the villagers knew it 'was good for the heart' and were preparing to boil up some leaves to make a soup for this purpose. However, information on its toxicity had not reached them, so they were advised against it; even in London at the end of the twentieth century, a librarian who made foxglove tea to treat his mother's intractable heart failure precipitated her sudden demise. When one considers that the tablets of dried foxglove leaf that were still being used to treat heart failure in the 1970s were smaller than a paracetamol tablet, it is easy to realise that only a small amount of leaf is required to be therapeutic, and more than that can be fatal.

Foxglove contains cardiac glycosides, in particular digoxin, which increase the strength of the heart's contractions and so increase cardiac output in heart failure. It is such a poisonous plant that it never appeared in any herbal until the middle of the sixteenth century when Leonard Fuchs (1542) published an account, with woodcuts, of *Digitalis purpurea* and *Digitalis lutea* (now *D. grandiflora*). He noted that it was bitter to taste and, quoting Galen, said that this indicated it was a purgative. Of course, Galen was correct, as most poisons taste bitter and most poisons cause diarrhoea and vomiting. One can but reflect on the lack of experimental evidence sought in the succeeding years, for Lyte (1578) and Gerard (1633) report that the leaves boiled in wine can be used to bring up phlegm and open the 'stoppings of the liver, spleen and mylte [spleen, again]'. It is clear that neither Fuchs, Lyte nor Gerard had tried it. Parkinson (1640) reports its use, additionally, for healing wounds, scrophula (tuberculosis of the lymph nodes in the neck) and epilepsy. Lobel does mention vomiting and purgation, but it disappears from herbals and pharmacopoeias until the mid-eighteenth century (James, 1752) when it is noted that 'the decoction of it purges very powerfully both upwards and downwards' i.e. causes profound vomiting and diarrhoea.

> When one considers that the tablets of dried foxglove leaf that were still being used to treat heart failure in the 1970s were smaller than a paracetamol tablet, it is easy to realise that only a small amount of leaf is required to be therapeutic, and more than that can be fatal.

The use of the purple foxglove, *D. purpurea*, for treating heart failure (then called 'dropsy') was uncovered by Dr William Withering (1785). One of his patients who was dying of terminal heart failure, for which he could do nothing, was treated by a Shropshire herbalist, Mrs Hutton, who had a secret remedy for dropsy which caused violent vomiting and purging. Withering was told the twenty or more herbs that were contained in the remedy and deduced that foxglove was the active ingredient. He experimented on his charity patients (those he treated for free) and gradually worked out that a small dose caused a diuresis and a large dose caused vomiting, and that the toxic effects accumulated – for the half-life of the active chemical, digoxin, in the body is about five days. He found that the leaves varied in strength according to the time of year and that the dry leaf was easier to use than an infusion or decoction. He found it did not work in women with fluid retention due to giant ovarian cysts, but in people with swollen legs and breathing difficulties it was effective. Withering recognised the toxic side effects of foxglove, including xanthopsia (objects appear yellow), bradycardia (slow pulse), vomiting and diarrhoea. He regarded it as a diuretic – the concept of increased cardiac output would take another century to appear.

Withering treated a patient, a Mrs Hill of Aston, who was under the care of Erasmus Darwin (the grandfather of Charles Darwin) and was very put out when Erasmus published the beneficial results of using foxglove in dropsy in this patient, in 1780. Despite this, Withering did not get round to publishing his findings until five years later in 1785, as *An Account of the Foxglove*.

*Digitalis purpurea* was used as *Dig. fol.* (tablets of dried digitalis leaves) until the 1960s. Pure digoxin was isolated from the leaves of *D. lanata* (the 'woolly' or 'Grecian' foxglove of Eastern Europe) in 1930 by Sydney Smith at Burroughs Wellcome.[26] This had the advantage of purity and not varying in strength according to the time of year. The LD50 (the minimum dose that would kill half a group of mice) was determined with each

harvest of dry foxglove leaves to ensure standard potency – unnecessary when pure digoxin could be measured in milligrams. Digoxin is still manufactured by extraction from *D. lanata.*

Currently digoxin is sometimes used in the treatment of atrial fibrillation, atrial flutter and, occasionally, for heart failure. While it was widely used in the UK for heart failure in the middle of the twentieth century, it was only licensed by the US Food and Drug Administration for this in 1998.

In the summer in the College Garden *Digitalis lanata* is visited by little *Anthidium manicatum* bees which become stuporose and lie upside down in the flowers, seeming unable to fly away when disturbed.

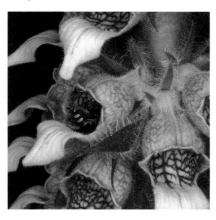

# CINCHONA

*Cinchona* L. Rubiaceae. Quinine.
Distribution: Western South America.

pecies of the genus *Cinchona* are the source of quinine, the drug of historic importance in the treatment of malaria. *Cinchona* does not grow in the College Garden because it is a tropical species but it is present on 192 of the 5800 sheets of the Pharmaceutical Society herbarium at the College.

The Quechua peoples of Peru, Bolivia and Ecuador used it for treating fevers. Woodville (1793) reports that its effects were said to have been discovered when *Cinchona* trees had fallen into a pool and made the water so bitter that no one would drink it, but a man afflicted with a violent fever and thirst was forced to drink it and was cured. It was named after the wife of the Spanish viceroy in Lima, Ana de Osorio, Countess of Chinchon, after she had been cured of a fever by an infusion of the bark in 1638.

Quinine, from *Cinchona*, was the first effective Western treatment for malaria

**It was named after the wife of the Spanish viceroy in Lima, Ana de Osorio, Countess of Chinchon, after she had been cured of a fever by an infusion of the bark in 1638.**

TOP and ABOVE: A bee, *Anthidium manicatum*, intoxicated by a flower of *Digitalis lanata*
RIGHT: *Cinchona* species from the herbarium of the Pharmaceutical Society herbarium at the College

Discovered by Mr R Thomson
in the central Cordillera of
the Colombian Andes

Cinchona "negra"
Cultivated, Bogotá
Mr R. Thomson

*Cinchona officinalis* in Peru

caused by *Plasmodium falciparum*, appearing in therapeutics in the seventeenth century when Bernabé Cobo (1582–1657) first brought *Cinchona* bark to Europe.

In England Robert Talbor, an English apothecary's apprentice, pioneered the use of *Cinchona* in the treatment of fevers, mostly due to malaria, in the seventeenth century (Talbor, 1672). He first used his secret remedy in the Fens and Essex where malaria was rife. When his cure was given to King Charles II and members of the European royalty, Talbor received a knighthood and was made Royal Physician. Quinine remained the antimalarial drug of choice until the 1940s, when other drugs such as chloroquine that have fewer unpleasant side effects replaced it. Because of the huge demand for *Cinchona* bark, and to maintain their monopoly, Peru and surrounding countries outlawed the export of *Cinchona* seeds and saplings, beginning in the early nineteenth century. In 1860, a British expedition to South America smuggled *Cinchona* seeds and plants, which were introduced to Darjeeling, India and Sri Lanka. By 1883, about 64,000 acres (260 sq. km) were in cultivation in Sri Lanka, with exports reaching a peak of 15 million pounds weight in 1886. Plantations were also established in Mexico to supply North America using seeds purchased from England. The Dutch government also smuggled seeds and by the 1930s Dutch plantations in Java were producing 22 million pounds of *Cinchona* bark, or 97% of the world's quinine production, annually.

A non-stereoselective quinine was synthesised from precursors in 1944 which led to more synthetic drugs that were able to control various stages of the disease. *Cinchona* bark remained the only source of quinine until 2001 when an effective stereoselective synthesis of quinine was devised, but this is not commercially viable.[67] Quinine is still extracted from *Cinchona* bark.

When his cure was given to King Charles II and members of the European royalty, Talbor received a knighthood and was made Royal Physician. Quinine remained the antimalarial drug of choice until the 1940s.

During World War II, Allied powers were cut off from their supply of quinine when the Germans conquered the Netherlands, where there were huge stockpiles, and the Japanese controlled the other sources of *Cinchona* bark in the Philippines and Indonesia. By December 1942, more than 8500 US soldiers were hospitalised with malaria. In one military hospital, 80% were infected.[67] The only other possible effective agent was Atabrine, but the troops would not take it as it was very toxic and was reputed to cause impotence.

Before the Japanese invasion of the Philippines, the United States had managed to obtain four million *Cinchona* seeds from there and planted them in Costa Rica. Unfortunately these supplies came too late and tens of thousands of Allied troops in Africa and the South Pacific died due to the lack of quinine. Even the Japanese did not make effective use of quinine and according to the US War Department (1943) every Japanese soldier in Burma had at least one attack of malaria.[83]

The alternative option was to return to South America to obtain *Cinchona* bark from where it originally grew. From 1942 onwards the US government sent teams of botanists and foresters to South America to find strains of *Cinchona* yielding high concentrations of quinine. This was difficult, not least because the various species of *Cinchona* interbreed and it was not obvious which were high-yielding hybrids. Many of these hybrids are represented in the College's Pharmaceutical Society herbarium. There were few natives skilled in stripping the bark and the teams suffered terrible privation as they had to penetrate deeper into jungles once the more accessible trees had been cut down. Nevertheless, by 1944, 12.5 million pounds of *Cinchona* bark had been shipped back to the USA.[67]

Quinine remains one of the recommended treatments for severe *Plasmodium falciparum* malaria, despite its toxicity and the availability of other agents such as Artesunate.

*Cinchona* bark also contains quinidine, a stereoisomer of quinine, used historically for the treatment of cardiac arrhythmias, first noted by the French physician Jean-Baptiste de Senac in 1749. Karel Wenckebach, immortalised by the Wenckebach phenomenon – an unusual type of irregular pulse – noted that one of his patients cured himself of atrial fibrillation by taking a gram of quinine, prepared from *Cinchona* bark. Its toxicity has caused it to fall out of favour.[27] Throughout the history of plant-based medicine, the discovery of separate chemicals with diverse uses from one source has been the rule rather than the exception.

ABOVE: *Artemisia annua*, Annual Wormwood. OPPOSITE: Flower of *Artemisia annua*

# ARTEMISIA ANNUA

***Artemisia annua*** L. Asteraceae. Sweet or Annual Wormwood; qīnghāosu or huanghuahao. Distribution: Temperate Asia, but naturalised worldwide.

During the Vietnam War, Ho Chi Minh asked the Chinese leader Mao Zhe Dong and Premier Zhou En Lai for help in treating malaria as it was harming many Vietcong soldiers. A secret programme – Project 523 – was established, and searching ancient records of Traditional Chinese Medicine revealed that an extract of *Artemisia annua* had been used since at least the third century CE to treat 'fevers' (as well as haemorrhoids).[40] The history of the subsequent identification and development of the active principle is disputed, but skilled chemical, biological and clinical work showed that the active principle was artemisinin, a novel sesquiterpene lactone with a 1,2,4-trioxane ring system (endoperoxide), which had great potency and unusual speed of action against malaria. Its development was subsequently replicated in the West and now several semi-synthetic derivatives have become the worldwide basis for combination therapies for the safe treatment of acute and recurrent malarial infections – artemether for oral and parenteral administration and artesunate for oral and rectal dosing. For twenty years the artemisinins have been the universal mainstay of the treatment particularly of acute *P. falciparum* malaria, the most severe and the most common form of the disease in Africa and Asia. Worryingly,

In the past decade there has been great interest in the very selective cytotoxic action of the artemisinins against many types of tumour cells and there are numerous ongoing trials of them to treat melanomas and cancers of the lung and stomach.

although still effective in many parts of the world, overuse and misuse has led to the development of resistant strains of *Plasmodium* in southeastern Asia – and increasingly in Africa and South America – so there is now an increasingly urgent search for new treatments for malaria.[89]

This hardy annual herb is native to east Asia and has been successfully naturalised throughout the world. The yield of artemisinin from the dried stems and leaves varies according to locale and climate, which has made its commercial cultivation as the source of the drugs a costly resource, whereas treatment of vast numbers of people in less-developed countries requires a low-cost drug. For a long while the only source was a precursor extracted from commercially cultivated *A. annua* in Guangzhou, China. The yield was limited, as programmes of selective plant improvement were incomplete. Several attempts to establish a local industry in Africa failed due to poor organisation and other local problems. An economically viable synthesis by a semisynthetic route has recently been introduced, based on extraction of a precursor, artemisinic acid, which is produced in much larger quantities than artemisinin by *A. annua*; its adoption by large companies should relieve concern about the future availability of this essential class of medicines. The artemisinin family of compounds does occur in other species of *Artemisia* but their concentration has been too low to support industrial cultivation and extraction (Dalrymple, 2012).

The endoperoxide molecular structure of the artemisinins and the potency and speed of its action against *Plasmodium*

has stimulated several drug discovery programmes, which have now produced leads in clinical trial, as well as other types of compounds.[10] The general scientific and public health concern about malaria has also led to the founding of a unique public–private partnership to promote research and development of treatments for this disease – Medicines for Malaria Venture (http://www.mmv.org) – a novel approach being adopted for several other diseases of the developing world.

In the past decade there has been great interest in the very selective cytotoxic action of the artemisinins against many types of tumour cells and there are numerous ongoing trials of them to treat melanomas and cancers of the lung and stomach.[28] The ability of physicians and pharmacists to find new uses for medicines continues unabated.

# DIOSCOREA BATATAS

**Dioscorea batatas**. Decne. Dioscoreaceae. Chinese yam. Distribution: China, east Asia.

 ams are perennial herbaceous vines, most with fleshy tubers. They are of medicinal importance in several distinct ways. The tubers of several species (mainly *Dioscorea rotundata, esculenta, cayenensis, opposita* and *trifida*) are widely cultivated for food, particularly in Africa and the Pacific region. They have been collected and grown for several thousand years as a productive and convenient source of edible starch and some protein, for ease of cooking and, unlike the increasingly popular cassava, most cultivated species are non-toxic and can be eaten with little preparation. Their use as food accounts for most of the rising world production, which had reached 60 million tonnes by 2013. Their abundance and ease of cultivation has contributed significantly to the world's population explosion.

The historical significance of the genus name *Dioscorea* lies in its commemoration of Pedanius Dioscorides of Anazarbus (40–90CE), the Greek physician and herbalist who published the first systematic account of the medicinal nature and uses of plants in ca. 70CE. His *De Materia Medica* is the precursor and, in many ways still the basis, of modern pharmacopoeias.

*Dioscorea batatas* is one of the few species used directly in herbal medicine; the cooked tuberous root from plants collected in the wild is considered in Traditional Chinese medicine to stimulate the stomach and spleen and to have a tonic action on the kidneys and lungs. Juice from the leaf is applied externally to treat snake bites and scorpion stings.

Other species of yam (*D. composita, D. mexicana* and *D. villosa*), collected from the wild as industrial cultivation was difficult, were of greater initial importance in the development of many medically valuable steroids, both corticosteroids and sex steroids, including anti-inflammatory glucocorticoids, oestrogens and gestagens, used as such, and as components of oral contraceptives. They have been displaced by the suitability of *D. batatas* for large-scale farming.

The identification, characterisation and pharmacology of steroids and chemical derivatives of them, and their subsequent large-scale manufacture and introduction into medicine, has a lengthy history of complexity, chemical feats, commercial coups and cantankerous

TOP: Artist's impression of Dioscorides of Anazarbus (40–90CE) from Elizabeth Blackwell's *A Curious Herbal* (1739)
ABOVE: *Dioscorea* aff. *batatas* in the College Garden

TOP: *Dioscorea mexicana* is a vigorous climbing vine
ABOVE: Tuber of *Dioscorea mexicana*, from which steroids were synthesised

developers. It has been driven more by industrial chemists of striking brilliance and entrepreneurial independence than by Nobel-prize winning academic biologists, chemists and physicians.

In the 1930s total synthesis of natural hormones or their extraction from animal sources was very difficult. Russell Marker, an American organic chemist, devised a theoretical route for the cheap, large-scale synthesis of progesterone in 1940–41. Several major US pharmaceutical companies refused to support his work on sex steroids (because they did not wish to be involved with contraception) so he funded his own small laboratory in Mexico City. After successfully and cheaply preparing kilograms of progesterone in 1943, which had previously only been available in grams and at high cost, he, Carl Djerassi (a Bulgarian–American chemist) and two Mexican colleagues founded a new company to continue to develop and manufacture several steroid hormones. Brilliant work in the 1940s and 50s by them and Percy Julian[96] (an American research chemist) showed how to make large quantities of the natural steroids and chemical analogues with better properties, from chemicals obtained from plants. The first successes came from converting stigmasterol, a waste product from soy bean processing, into cortisone. This was soon followed by use of diosgenin from the Mexican yam *Dioscorea mexicana*, and later hecogenin from sisal (*Agave sisalana*) waste to manufacture progesterone and other sex steroids. Plant-derived materials are still the basis of steroid industries in many countries, although the modern trend of using biochemically engineered lower organisms for industrial production of chemicals is displacing both collection from the wild and the harvesting of cultivated plants. At least one hundred million women now take a contraceptive pill to try to control the population explosion that this plant, as a cheap source of food, contributed so much to causing in the first place.

# ARUNDO DONAX, HORDEUM VULGARE

**Arundo donax** L. Poaceae. Giant or Spanish Reed. Distribution: Central and southern Asia.

**Hordeum vulgare** L. Poaceae. Barley. Distribution: North Africa, Asia, Europe.

 he fast-growing *Arundo donax* has been cultivated in the Mediterranean area for many thousands of years. Its medical and cultural significance comes from several different historical uses.[56] The ancient Egyptians used it to wrap the dead before burial; and its ability to concentrate arsenic from ground water may be useful in remediation of contaminated land, as in Bangladesh. More generally there is interest in it as a very efficient biomass plant for use as a fuel, and its stiffness makes it useful in constructing simple buildings. It is still used as the reed in the oboe, bassoon, clarinet, saxophone and bagpipe and has been used to make Pan pipes. Its use for musical instruments goes back to the classical era, when it was used to make flutes and whistles.

The history of Barley (*Hordeum vulgare*), is just as ancient, as it has been eaten by humans in the Fertile Crescent for at least 10,000 years.[4] It is described as a currency in the Code of Hammurabi in 1700BCE and is mentioned in the Bible (Exodus 9:31, Ezekiel 4:9 and Ruth 1:22). In the reign of Edward II (1284–1327) three grains of Barley laid end to end made up the official inch (=2.5cm). We

Lidocaine and the reeds for wind instruments can be sourced from *Arundo donax*, the Giant Reed

Barley, *Hordeum vulgare*, was the original source of lidocaine and, when infected with ergot fungus, of ergometrine

**In the Middle Ages Europe was ravaged by epidemics of St Anthony's fire, caused by eating bread made from contaminated rye. Hallucinations, tingling and burning were followed by gangrene.**

grow the domesticated six-row Barley (a mutant form with seeds arranged in triplets in two rows). Culpeper calls it 'French Barley', listing its uses (following Dioscorides, Galen and Hippocrates) as 'cooling, nourishing and breeds milk'. Gerard (1633) notes that French Barley was the variety without husks (now *Hordeum vulgare* var. *nudum*) and was particularly good for making a ptisane (Barley water) 'a noble drink for sick folks'. He adds that Barley meal was used to make up poultices when mixed with other plants, such as garden poppy (*Papaver somniferum*); garden nightshade (*Solanum nigrum*); Fenugreek (*Trigonella foenum-graecum*); Linseed (*Linum usitatissimum*); and hog's grease – in this case for hot swellings and dropsy. It was used by the College in 1618 as mentioned in its *Pharmacopoeia Londinensis*.

Numerous cultivars have been developed, with about half of world production being used as animal feed and a quarter for beer production. Infection with the fungus *Claviceps purpurea* which produces ergometrine, had been known since 600BCE, when an Assyrian tablet mentioned a 'noxious pustule in the ear of grain'. In the Middle Ages Europe was ravaged by epidemics of St Anthony's fire, caused by eating bread made from contaminated rye. Hallucinations, tingling and burning were followed by gangrene. This was caused by ergot alkaloids: lysergic acid derivatives and derivatives of 6,8-dimethylergoline such as ergotoxine, ergotamine and ergometrine. By the eighteenth century powdered ergot was known as '*pulvis ad partum*' (Latin for 'powder for delivery') and was used for prolonged labour. But soon it was realised that the uterine contractions that it caused were so powerful that it was too dangerous to use before the child was born. However, ergometrine may be life-saving in controlling *post-partum* haemorrhage, which is often due to the failure of the uterus to contract after delivery. In the 1930s ergometrine was isolated by Dudley in Oxford and was shown to cause contraction of the human *post-partum* uterus by Chassar Moir in London. Before 1940 the maternal death rate from *post-partum* haemorrhage was three per 10,000 deliveries, but in the 1950s, with the use of ergometrine, the maternal death rate from PPH had fallen five-fold to 0.6 per 10,000 deliveries.

The connection of these two plants with the local anaesthetic lidocaine is clear but tortuous. The starting point in lidocaine's discovery came from research in Sweden by Hans von Euler in the early 1920s. He was interested in the possibility of developing an agricultural nematocide based on his studies of a mutant, chlorophyll deficient, nematode-resistant Barley, which he showed was due to its content of *gramine*. Misdirected synthesis of that in the early 1930s, by a young assistant, Holger Erdtman, led to *isogramine,* which was found to numb the tongue and lips when tasted, a common but very misguided habit of chemists. More focused structure-activity work on that amino-amide molecule by Nils Löfgren led to the synthesis of lidocaine in 1943. A switch away from initial testing on himself by a pharmacology student, Bengt Lundqvist, to formal investigations in animals and subsequently in humans with the help of medical contacts amongst Lundqvists fellow Swedish fencers, led to its development by Astra AB and Sweden's first specialist anaesthetist, Torsten Gordh, as a powerful and safe local anaesthetic. Lidocaine's activity as a Class Ib anti-arrhythmic drug was recognised in 1972. The mechanism of the local anaesthetic and anti-arrhythmic activities of lidocaine involves its inhibition of sodium channels by binding to specific sites in the channels in the membranes of nerves and other excitable cells.[59]

Gramine, which is toxic and causes neurological disorders in high doses, is naturally plentiful in *Arundo,* as in many other plants. This gave rise to an alternative and more exciting but inaccurate story linking the discovery of lidocaine to the observation in Asiatic Russia that not even camels from Turkestan would eat the canes. Investigations by two Russian chemists, Orechoff and Norkina,[55] two years after von Euler, led them independently to the isolation of gramine from *Arundo donax*, which they called donaxin. They did not take it further to develop a local anaesthetic. As Arthur Hollman has noted, the story of the camels and *Arundo donax* was a good one, but not relevant to the discovery of lidocaine. However, a local anaesthetic effect seems to have been known nearly 2000 years earlier, for Dioscorides notes of the juice of *Arundo*: 'it soothes sprains and pains on the lower part of the back when plastered on with vinegar' as well as being a treatment for 'erysipelas and other inflammations'. The latter might encompass the post-herpetic neuralgia for which lignocaine patches have been found to be so useful.

# POISONOUS PLANTS WHICH HAVE CHANGED THE WORLD

This section acts as a reminder that plants have spent 370 million years on the planet and over that time have developed very impressive toxins and a myriad ways to kill predators. These are just some examples, some surprising, some well-known, which have killed or maimed tens of thousands and even millions. While there are plenty with lethal toxins, such as the euphorbias, most are only known to have killed occasionally. Even the most benign-looking of garden plants, our *Rhododendron*, it is alleged, has been responsible for thousands of deaths, and its infamy has gone down in history. However, while wonderfully toxic, all allegations (some ancient, some recent) of it as the source of poisonous honey which drove classical armies mad may be a case of mistaken identity, and we will argue that the culprit is Oleander, a shrub known as *Rhododendron* until relatively recently.

## NICOTIANA TABACUM, NICOTIANA RUSTICUM

**Nicotiana tabacum** L. Solanaceae. Tobacco, *Herba Sancta, Nicotiana*. Distribution: originally from Latin America, now worldwide.

**Nicotiana rustica** L. Solanaceae. Aztec Tobacco, *Hyoscyamus luteus*, *Hyoscyamus tertius*, *Tabacum minus, Petume* or Petun. Distribution: Latin America.

 icotiana tabacum has to be the world's most poisonous plant, causing the premature death of six million people every year (that is one person every five seconds, you can do the maths); and expected to rise to seven million by 2020 and to eight million by 2030 – that is ten times more than malaria. No other plant 'causes lung cancer,

ABOVE: Flowers of *Nicotiana tabacum*, tobacco
LEFT: *Nicotiana tabacum*, tobacco

TOP: The first illustration of tobacco, *Nicotiana tabacum*, with a man smoking (Pena & Lobel, 1570)
ABOVE: First illustration of *Nicotiana rustica*. as *Hyoscyamus luteus* (Dodoens, 1554)

respiratory disease and heart disease as well as numerous cancers in other organs including lip, mouth, throat, bladder, kidney, stomach, liver and cervix' – and that is just listing the common illnesses (ASH Fact Sheet on Smoking and Health).[3] It contains little of the tropane alkaloids, like atropine, that feature so strongly in other members of the Solanaceae, nicotine being its major biologically active alkaloid. Enough nicotine can be absorbed from fresh leaves through the skin of workers handling the crop in wet weather to cause nicotine poisoning. It is of course a wonderful insecticide, produced millennia of evolutionary time, and the aphids which are placed by ants on the plants of *Nicotiana rustica* in the College Garden die almost immediately, so the stems become littered with their corpses.

Up to nine million tons of the leaf of *N. tabacum* are made into cigarettes annually; 1.1 billion people smoke nearly 6000 billion cigarettes per year. This is a successful plant. It all began (for us) 500 years ago in 1518 when the RCP was founded. It was then that Friar Ramon Pané introduced the seeds from Mexico to Spain. He had previously sailed on Columbus's second voyage to the New World and brought back snuff in 1496. Seeds of *N. rustica* were brought to England in 1565 by Sir John Hawkins and of *N. tabacum* by Sir Francis Drake in 1575 (Winter, 2000). It is a salutary reflection that a plant which came into Europe in the year the

**It is a salutary reflection that a plant which came into Europe in the year the College was founded became the single greatest cause of disease that its Members and Fellows have to deal with. It is an indictment that it took over 400 years before this was realised.**

College was founded became the single greatest cause of disease that its Members and Fellows have to deal with. It is an indictment that it took over 400 years before this was realised.[16,18] It bears repeating what we now all know from the publication by Richard Doll and Austin Bradford Hill (1954) that 'mild smokers were seven times more likely to die of lung cancer as non-smokers, and immoderate smokers are 24 times more likely'.[16,17,18]

The history of tobacco is too long to tell here, so we will give you a few snippets from the Dorchester Library to illustrate the spread of knowledge of its names, appearance and uses. *Nicotiana rustica* first appears as a woodcut as *Hyoscyamus luteus* in Dodoens (1554) and he has a good woodcut of *N. tabacum* as *Hyoscyamus peruvianus* in 1583. The credit for the first image of someone smoking goes to the Flemish physician and botanist Matthias de L'Obel and his friend Pierre Pena (Lobel and Pena, 1570). They published a lovely woodcut of a plant of *N. tabacum* with a man smoking from an enormously long, narrowly conical tube made of leaves – for which the local name was a 'tobaco' (sic). There is a long discussion about 'tobaco' ending with praise for it being the best thing to have come out of the New World. Also discussed are the similarities that its leaves had to *Symphytum* (comfrey), and the flowers and seeds to *Hyoscyamus* (Henbane), but distinguishing it from *Hyoscyamus luteus* (i.e. from *N. rusticum*). Lobel and Pena extolled its use for everything from wounds to chest problems and explained how smoking it causes exhilaration and inebriation. They call it *Herba sancta* (Holy plant), because of its reputed properties as a panacea, and *Nicotiana* after Jean Nicot, the Portuguese ambassador who introduced it to Catherine de' Medici in 1560 as a treatment for her migraine. A second illustration of *N. rustica* appears with a woodcut as *Hyoscyamus tertius* (Matthiolus, 1569) and as *Herba sancta sive* [or] *Tabacum minus* and *Santa sancta, sive Tabacum minimum* (L'Obel, 1576). He writes: 'It mollifies the pain of teeth which have been caused by cold

TOP: *Nicotiana rustica* growing wild in its native Peru
ABOVE: Flowers of *Nicotiana rustica*

plants. The syrup and juice, or drops in water in a measuring spoon alleviate asthma and orthopnoea [shortness of breath on lying flat].' It was probably Nicolás Monardes (1512–88), a Spanish physician, who did as much as anyone to popularise its medical use in this country, with his great lists of beneficial uses in all sorts of diseases (Monardes, 1577). We commemorate him by growing *Monarda didyma* in the College Garden. There were many other names given to these two plants and William Piso (1648), who saw it growing in Brazil, illustrates *N. tabacum* under the name *Petúme* or *Tabacum* and *Petum* with a diatribe against its assumed medicinal benefits. Few heeded the warning.

Cigarettes are also a nuisance in the Garden and with discreet notices we try to discourage smokers from using the flower beds as ashtrays.

# ARISTOLOCHIA CLEMATITIS

**Aristolochia clematitis** L. Aristolochiaceae. Birthwort. Distribution: Mediterranean, Asia. Name in the *Pharmacopoeia Londinensis* (1618) was 'Aristolochia'.

 ristolochia clematitis, Birthwort, is the plant which made the world aware of the dangers of the unregulated use of traditional herbal medicines – the herbalists' equivalent of the thalidomide disaster for allopathic medicines, and which resulted in international legislation. This plant is a wonderful example of the Doctrine of Signatures but a potent cause of renal failure and cancer of the upper urinary tract. The flower of Birthwort looks like the female lower genital tract, hence the recommendation of Dioscorides to use it in childbirth to help expel the placenta. We grow it in the Garden to remind us of its old associations and modern dangers – not unique in being an oncogenic plant, but it is one which has caused renal tract cancers worldwide.

Gerard (1633) recommended *Aristolochia* primarily for snake bite but also says that others use it for plague, smallpox and measles. Pliny used it for cramp, convulsions and bruises; as an aid for labour; and for guaranteeing a male child if applied topically to a newly pregnant woman. He says it was called 'poison of the earth' by fishermen, who found that the crushed root, made into pellets, with lime was an irresistible bait for fish, 'but no sooner had they tasted thereof, but they will turne up their bellies, and lie floating aloft upon the water starke dead'. At the time of the College's *Pharmacopoeia*, Culpeper wrote of *A. clematitis*: 'being drunk in Wine, brings away both birth and afterbirth and whatever a careless Midwife hath left behind'. Obstetric mishaps occurred even then.

Modern science has found that *Aristolochia clematitis* contains aristolochic acid, which can cause kidney failure and cancer of the urinary tract. This effect is so serious that in 2001 the FDA advised producers, physicians and consumers to immediately discontinue use of any botanical products containing aristolochic acid.[21] The potential sources were

OPPOSITE: *Aristolochia clematitis*, widely used in herbal medicine until it was found to cause renal failure and cancer of the urinary tract, so now banned worldwide

Pliny used it for cramp, convulsions and bruises; as an aid for labour; and for guaranteeing a male child if applied topically to a newly pregnant woman.

*Aristolochia clematitis*, the cause of Balkan endemic nephropathy

## It seems very likely that aristolochic acid is the causative factor in Balkan endemic nephropathy.

widened to 'any botanical products' because there are at least 500 other species of *Aristolochia*, all of which may contain aristolochic acid. More importantly, Traditional Chinese Medicines (TCM) were identified, in which the roots of *Aristolochia fangchi* were substituted for *Stephania tetrandra*, as in the product being sold as 'Stephania', a slimming aid. The result of the FDA ban on *Aristolochia* products led the way to many European Medicine agencies controlling all herbal preparations more rigorously.

The possible connection between *Aristolochia* and renal failure first came to light in the 1950s, when a high incidence of a specific form of renal failure was noted, first in Bulgaria and then in Yugoslavia and Romania.[73] This was an interstitial nephritis, which was only manifest in adults and developed very slowly. It became known as the Balkan nephropathy. Since the Balkan nephropathy was only found in the country and not in towns and was confined to certain villages, an environmental factor was suspected. Kazantizis first suggested that the problem was bread baked from flour that had been contaminated by *A. clematitis*.[34] Ivic, in a series of field observations in the South Morava region of Serbia, found that it was indeed widespread in the wheat fields.[32] Even though the seeds of *A. clematitis* are not necessarily ripe when the wheat is harvested, it seems very likely that aristolochic acid is the causative factor in Balkan endemic nephropathy, even if the precise mechanism whereby the agent is transmitted from *A. clematitis* is disputed. Skin absorption in field workers and smoke inhalation from burning fields were alternatives suggested.[38] There may also be a genetic basis towards the development of *Aristolochia*-induced nephrotoxicity as not all the villagers were affected.

The association between *Aristolochia* and TCM came when Vanherweghem (1993), a Belgian nephrologist, noted that two of his female patients with a rapidly developing interstitial nephritis had both been taking Chinese herbal preparations as part of a weight-loss programme.[85] One hundred and five of approximately 1800 women attending the TCM clinic for weight loss developed end-stage renal disease requiring dialysis and/or renal transplantation. Several subsequently developed cancer of the upper urinary tract related to the total dose of aristolochic acid consumed.[52] The TCM herbal substance was sold as 'Stephania'. It contained *A. fangchi* instead of *Stephania tetrandra*. This was not necessarily deceitful; it is common practice to make such substitutions in TCM, and the TCM practitioners may have believed that the root of *A. fangchi* was just as effective as that of *Stephania tetrandra*.[20] The fact that 'only' 105 of 1800 women exposed to *Aristolochia*-contaminated Stephania developed renal failure reinforces the suggestion that there is a genetic susceptibility to *Aristolochia*-induced nephrotoxicity.

In the UK the MHRA in 2002 issued a position statement entitled *Safety of Herbal Medicinal Products* 'in response to a request from Members of Parliament and herbal interest groups for background information to inform discussions on the proposed EU Directive on Traditional Herbal Medicinal Products'. This flowed from legislation – The Medicines (Aristolochia and Mu Tong etc.) (Prohibition) Order 2001 – which prohibited herbal use of *Aristolochia* species and a number of other herbal ingredients which can be confused with, or substituted for, *Aristolochia*, in unlicensed medicine.[77] The European Medicines Agency issued a similar statement in 2005 commenting that most EU Member States had taken regulatory action to protect the public from unlicensed medicines containing toxic *Aristolochia* species.[20]

# ARGEMONE MEXICANA

**Argemone mexicana** L. Papaveraceae. Mexican poppy, Mexican prickly poppy. In India it is called Satyanashi, meaning 'devastating'. Distribution: Western USA, West Indies and Mexico.

 exico is the country of origin of this invasive species, tolerant of drought and poor soils, which has become naturalised all round the world. Its silver-veined leaves and butter-yellow flowers make it an attractive plant on rockeries and it is 'low maintenance' as it self-seeds so readily. It contains sanguinarine and dihydrosanguinarine, produced in the plant and stored in the rhizome, but not the opiate alkaloids found in other members of its family. Sanguinarine is found in several Papaveraceae, including *Chelidonium majus, Sanguinaria canadensis* and *Macleaya cordata,* and in the herbaceous parts of *Papaver somniferum* (but not the seed capsule). Its poisonous properties are simple – it kills animal cells. Less simply, it kills animal cells by poisoning the sodium– potassium pump which maintains cell membrane function. This property has led to it being investigated for anti-cancer properties and being made into 'black paste' by US herbalists for the treatment of basal cell carcinomas (rodent ulcers) of the face. Sanguinarine destroys the cells with which it comes into contact, but the cell death

Mexican poppy, *Argemone mexicana*, has caused Epidemic Dropsy from Nepal to South Africa

extends far beyond the initial area of contact. An internet photo of a woman who had used 'black paste' showed a noseless face half eaten away by a huge black eschar (scab). A chemical which kills animal cells also kills bacterial cells, and this 'natural' antibacterial chemical led to its former use in the Viadent range of toothpastes and mouthwashes. The discovery that users were nine times more likely to develop oral leukoplakia – a precancerous condition – is a caution against regarding natural products as harmless.

It is by the contamination – and often deliberate adulteration – of mustard seed used to make cooking oil that *Argemone* seed has caused real havoc. The seeds yield 35% argemone (aka katkar) oil, which has high concentrations of sanguinarine and dihydrosanguinarine. Mustard oil (used for cooking in India and elsewhere), contaminated with as little as 1% katkar oil, has caused numerous outbreaks of a condition called Epidemic Dropsy, affecting thousands of people in India,

Mauritius, Fiji, Madagascar, South Africa and Nepal. The cell damage results in proteinuria and consequent hypoalbuminaemia with fluid retention, pitting oedema and congestive cardiac failure, renal failure, anaemia, skin pigmentation, retinal haemorrhages, glaucoma and shortness of breath. There is also extensive depletion of antioxidants, especially vitamins E and A (tocopherol and retinol). The death rate is 5%, but with symptomatic treatment recovery usually occurs within three months. In these countries the mustard seed used for cooking-oil production is *Brassica juncea*, whose seeds are brown and difficult to distinguish from the black *Argemone* seeds. Farmers are encouraged to grow yellow-seeded mustard so contamination can easily be detected when the seeds are inspected prior to oil extraction. The yellow-seed mustard is *Sinapis alba* which has a lower oil content (24–35%) than the others (up to 43%), but the safety is an advantage. It is suggested that *Brassica campestris* (the source of rape seed oil) is used, but this also has brown/ black seeds so has the same problem as *B. juncea*. Yellow-seed mustard oil does not mix well with *Argemone* oil so can also be detected at the oil stage. Contamination of wheat flour in South Africa with the seeds of *A. mexicana* caused the same illness.

Plants evolve poisons to deter predators and as a growing plant *A. mexicana* is very successful. Its corrosive sap makes it something no animal or mollusc would try twice. Problems begin after it is harvested and its chemicals extracted and mixed with edible products, making clear the importance of legislation and vigilance against food adulteration.

The seeds of *Argemone mexicana* are the source of the poisonous katkar oil

Mustard oil (used for cooking in India and elsewhere), contaminated with as little as 1% katkar oil, has caused numerous outbreaks of a condition called Epidemic Dropsy, affecting thousands of people

# RHODODENDRON YAKUSHIMANUM

**Rhododendron yakushimanum** Nakai. Ericaceae. Distribution: Yakushima, Japan.

akushima is an island off the south coast of Japan where this plant was discovered in the early 1900s. It was introduced to the UK in 1934. It is found growing from sea level to 1000 metres and the higher altitude, cold-tolerant plants are those we grow in our British gardens today. They form beautiful curved mounds of closely packed leathery leaves which are dusted with a white indumentum above and brown below. These become almost invisible when covered in pink flowers in spring. We grow it as it is a nice, small *Rhododendron* with a vicious poison, representing a genus much maligned as the source of the honey which poisoned three armies of the classical era. We tell the story here to refute the calumny to which it has been subjected, arguing that the honey was poisoned by the pollen of Oleander (*Nerium oleander*), which was called *Rhododendron* until comparatively recently (Linnaeus, 1753).

*Rhododendrons have no medicinal value but the leaves are very poisonous due to a toxic resin called grayanotoxin. This is a neurotoxin which blocks sodium channels in cell membranes and receptors, leaving cells depolarised.*

Rhododendrons have no medicinal value but the leaves are very poisonous due to a toxic resin called grayanotoxin. This is a neurotoxin which blocks sodium channels in cell membranes and receptors, leaving cells depolarised. Grayanotoxin is also present in the nectar of the flowers; sucking it from the flowers, or eating as little as two leaves, can be fatal.

Honey from *Rhododendron ponticum* is said to have poisoned Xenophon's retreating army of 10000 men in 401BCE, as grayanotoxin in the nectar became incorporated into the honey. In the account in his *Anabasis* (CAIS, 1998–2015), Xenophon tells how his army, having defeated the Colchians near Trebizond in Pontus (modern day Anatolia), came to a village.[8] He writes:

*Now for the most part there was nothing here which they really found strange; but the swarms of bees in the neighbourhood were numerous, and the soldiers who ate of the honey all went off their heads, and suffered from vomiting and diarrhoea, and not one of them could stand up, but those who had eaten a little were like people exceedingly drunk, while those who had eaten a great deal seemed like crazy, or even, in some cases, dying men. So they lay there in great numbers as though the army had suffered a defeat, and great despondency prevailed. On the next day, however, no one had died, and at approximately the same hour as they had eaten the honey they began to come to their senses; and on the third or fourth day they got up, as if from a drugging.*

OPPOSITE: *Rhododendron yakushimanum* – a much maligned genus with a potent neurotoxin

Xenophon makes no mention of *Rhododendron*. There is a problem anyway on blaming this on grayanotoxin, the symptoms of which are given as 'excessive salivation, perspiration, vomiting, dizziness, weakness and paresthesia in the extremities and around the mouth, low blood pressure, sinus bradycardia and heart block. In higher doses symptoms can include loss of coordination, severe and progressive muscular weakness'. Delirium, 'madness' and 'going off their heads' is not reported. While cases of 'mad honey' poisoning are still reported from Turkey, analysis for the presence of *Rhododendron* pollen or grayanotoxins in the honey, or grayanotoxin levels in the patients, needs to be done for verification.

Pliny blames Oleander. He writes:

> **Another kind of honey there is in the same region of Pontus, … which because it driveth folk into a fit of rage and madnesse, they call in Greek Maenomenon. Some attribute (this) … to the flower of the Oleander, whereof the woods and forests there be full.**

He says of the name 'Oleander' (*Nerium oleander*): '…the Oleander … cometh from the Greeks, as may appear by the name Rhododendron. Some call it Nerion; others Rhododaphne …'. He describes how poisonous it is to animals. Dioscorides concurs.

The symptoms of Oleander poisoning include diarrhoea and vomiting, weakness, low blood pressure, fainting, confusion and disorientation, which are the symptoms experienced by Xenophon's soldiers.

Before the mid-eighteenth century, *Rhododendron* was the name for the shrub which we now call Oleander (*Nerium oleander*) with Oleander, Nerium and other names as synonyms. True *Rhododendron* was not known to early writers. The herbals of Fuchs (1542); Matthiolus (1569); Pena and Lobel (1570); Dodoens (1583); Pliny (1634); Parkinson (1640) and Bauhin (1680), in writing of *Rhododendron*, illustrate it with a woodcut of Oleander, *Nerium oleander*. It is clear that for 2000 years scholars understood that Pompey had been poisoned by honey from the plant we call Oleander, which they called *Rhododendron*.

The great botanist Sir Joseph Hooker (1855) noted that the honey from the wild bees of East Nepal was much sought after, 'except in spring when it is said to be poisoned by *Rhododendron* flowers, just as that eaten by the soldiers in the retreat of the Ten Thousand [i.e. Xenophon's army], was by the flowers of the R[hododendron] ponticum'. Whether it was Hooker who first blamed *R. ponticum*, because it was found in (and named for) Pontus, as the culprit, it matters not.

*Rhododendron* has a defence. Since the introduction of *R. ponticum* to England 250 years ago it has become an invasive weed, carpeting vast areas of hillside and woodland. It has never given rise to a case of 'mad honey', despite having bees which visit it and apparently become stupefied by it. It is also abundant in the USA and no cases have been reported there. This may, of course, be because it flowers in June and honey produced before then is used by bees for their larvae and what we consume is harvested later in the year and separated from pollen-containing brood honey. But if bees produce honey in the spring in East Nepal from *Rhododendron* there will be grayanotoxin contamination in the honey that could affect the Nepalese if it were collected and eaten.

The story by Strabo (c. 63BCE–24CE) in his *Geographica* (Hamilton & Falconer, 1903) of mad honey poisoning Pompey's (106–48BCE) soldiers is often mis-told. It relates the story of the Byzeres, a tribe from the seven villages (called the 'Heptacometæ') on the eastern side of Pontus, who were particularly savage. They lived in trees or small towers and:

> *... attack travellers, leaping down from the floors of their dwellings among the trees. The Heptacometæ cut off three of Pompey's cohorts [i.e. 1440 men, as a cohort = 480 men approximately] as they were passing through the mountains, by placing on their road vessels filled with maddening honey, which is procured from the branches of trees. The men who had tasted the honey and lost their senses were attacked and easily despatched.*

There is no mention of *Rhododendron* or Oleander, but it is clear that this honey was from wild honeycombs.

Magor's (1990) story that honey from *R. afghanicum* poisoned Alexander the Great's army in 327BCE while he was on his way to conquer India appears to be a corruption of Xenophon's story.[43] The fantastic stories of Alexander's encounters, full of weird half-men half-animals, in McCrindle's biography of Alexander would surely have noted it if it had been recorded.[46]

So, a brief note on *Nerium oleander*:

# NERIUM OLEANDER

***Nerium oleander*** L. Apocynaceae. Oleander. Distribution: Mediterranean to Western China.

 eautiful and elegant, this tender shrub, with small dog rose-like flowers, is grown in pots outside William Harvey House, where it has enough shelter to survive the winter. All parts of the plant contain cardiac glycosides, with a narrow therapeutic index. Ingestion results in diarrhoea and vomiting, weakness, low blood pressure, fainting, confusion and disorientation terminating in bradycardia and cardiac arrest. The specific chemical is oleandrin, causing inhibition of the sodium pump, in the same manner as digoxin from foxgloves. Like many poisonous plants, its toxins make it successful and, perhaps for this reason, it has never evolved into any other species within the genus. Nothing eats it normally, not even deer, and human cases of fatal poisoning are rare and usually the result of suicide. However, as commonly happens, an insect finds a way to make use of the poison to protect itself, and the caterpillar of the Australasian Common Crow butterfly (*Euploe core*) feeds on the leaves and becomes poisonous to birds. Animals eating dried fodder

containing *N. oleander* succumb and 100gm (3.5 ounces, in old measurements) is sufficient to kill a horse. Pliny reports that sheep and goats die if they drink water in which Oleander leaves have been soaked.

Folklore has a tendency to update urban myths. Reports that meat roasted on sticks made from Oleander has killed whole families having a barbeque and that some of Wellington's soldiers in the Peninsula war, and even soldiers in Alexander the Great's army, were killed in the same way, may just be the same story retold. It sounds entirely plausible but has been refuted by measurements of oleandrin in hot dogs cooked on Oleander skewers, which have shown negligible amounts of it[72] but smoke from burning it can be toxic.[30]

If we are to blame the nectar of Oleander as being the source of poisoned honey, it needs proof. Folklore blames the nectar of Oleander for poisoning honey and children who suck it from the flowers. Herrera[25] reports that Oleander flowers do not contain nectar and rely on deception for pollination – the flowers look (to a bee) as if they should contain nectar but do not. In Spain bees rarely visit the flowers, but they are bee-pollinated in the wild. If the specific bee pollinator does not occur in Spain, but is common in Pontus, significant amounts of pollen will be collected in Pontus. The pollen occurs in sticky lumps, which are taken back to the hive and stored as food for bee larvae. Modern honey producers separate the honey from the pollen/food cells in the honeycomb, so we do not eat significant amounts of pollen in our honey. However, people who eat wild honeycombs eat it all, so poisoning by honey containing Oleander pollen is perfectly possible.

So we present the very tentative hypothesis that the poisoning of Xenophon's men in 401BCE was due to eating honeycombs containing the pollen of *Nerium oleander*, not the nectar of *Rhododendron*, and that the error arose because for 2000 years, plants of *Nerium oleander* were called *Rhododendron*.

OPPOSITE and ABOVE: *Nerium oleander*, which may have poisoned the armies of Xenophon and Pompey

# MORE POISONOUS PLANTS, USES AND ABUSES

Here we will start with an important family of plants, the Solanaceae. Potatoes (*Solanum tuberosum*), tomatoes (*Lycopersicon esculentum*), chillies (*Capsicum annuum*) and aubergines (*Solanum melongena*) are among our staple foods. They are all poisonous except for the parts we actually eat. *Nicotiana tabacum,* as noted earlier, is our favourite poison. Other Solanaceae have medicinal value as the source of the tropane alkaloids: atropine, hyoscyamine and scopolamine. This short chapter tells the story of a novel local anaesthetic action discovered in the Garden from a plant which will let you jump the queue in the Accident and Emergency department. It also discusses another genus, which nearly killed John Gerard and a grandson, and does kill snails and rodent ulcers, and could be useful for leukaemia.

## BRUGMANSIA SUAVEOLENS

**Brugmansia suaveolens** (Willd.) Sweet. Solanaceae. Angels' Trumpets. Distribution: South America.

 s a highly decorative, night-fragrant, tender shrub, it is at its best from August to September, with its large hanging bells, in yellow and pink, in the planters on the Wolfson Terrace. Ours survives the winter on the Terrace, wrapped in fleece and against the warm, blue-brick walls of the College. *Brugmansia* used to be in the genus *Datura*, but can be distinguished by the hanging bells – the bell-shaped flowers of *Datura* point upwards.

Every part of *Brugmansia* – flowers, leaves, roots – contains high concentrations of the neuro-active tropane alkaloid scopolamine (hyoscine). This blocks the actions of the parasympathetic nervous system and in small doses dries up bronchial and salivary secretions, reduces gastric acid production and nausea, speeds up the heart rate, dilates the pupils and relaxes smooth muscle. In higher doses it causes disinhibition, hallucinations, coma, short-term memory loss and death. The combination of dry mouth and short-term memory loss may be thought a good reason for including it in preoperative 'premeds'. Inhalation of saliva is undesirable in an unconscious patient and although short-term memory loss may be desirable if one wakes up during an operation, the dose is likely to be too small to ensure the latter. It

OPPOSITE: *Brugmansia suaveolens* 'Grand Marnier' contains scopolamine

*Brugmansia suaveolens* 'Pink Beauty' is one of the several cultivars grown in the Garden

**Used in sea-sickness pills and patches and to treat intestinal and ureteric colic, and it reduces post-operative vomiting.**

is used in sea-sickness pills and patches and to treat intestinal and ureteric colic, and reduce post-operative vomiting. Like atropine, scopolamine will paralyse the pupillary light reflex, dilating the pupil. A professor of medicine visiting the College Garden noted that his grand-daughter had (in another place) been playing with the flowers of *Brugmansia* and given herself a dilated pupil when she touched her eye. As a unilateral dilated pupil when not due to 'gardener's mydriasis' (as this phenomenon is called), is a sign of same-sided brain compression we should remember it if one wishes to avoid the four-hour wait in A&E, as one sight of it should get a patient seen faster than one can say 'triage'.

Italians still grow *Brugmansia* beside their maize fields in Tuscany, for the large leaves were dried and smoked during World War II when tobacco was hard to come by. However, as the alkaloids are not destroyed by smoking, it is a safer way to induce hallucinations than drinking an unknown quantity as a tea – although not at all good for the lungs. It is easier to titrate the dose of hallucinogen by smoking as the effect is almost instantaneous and smoking ceases when 'enough' has been taken. It is reported that hallucinations induced by these alkaloids are not pleasant, although some ladies who ate Deadly Nightshade (*Atropa belladonna*) berries at the Chelsea Physic Garden a few years ago ended up in the Chelsea and Westminster Hospital with hallucinations for a week, but apparently enjoyed them.

Oil from the seeds is used topically to alleviate pain, a phenomenon that is not explained in the literature. However, one of the Garden Fellows, demonstrating the smell of the sap to a series of tour visitors over a weekend by rubbing the leaves with his thumb, index and middle fingers, found that the tips had become numb. They remained numb for three years, and now five years on have still not recovered their previous sensibility. Not a conventional local anaesthetic then, but presumably a toxin that damaged sensory neurones. The leaves were available on prescription as cigars, in the early years of the NHS, to relieve asthma, and these cigars can be seen in the Ethnobotany Department at the Royal Botanic Gardens, Kew. Whether they alleviated asthma, or just induced a frame of mind so that the patient no longer minded having asthma, is not reported. The ability of plant toxins to be absorbed through the skin is demonstrated by voodoo ladies in Haiti who rub themselves with the leaves until a trance state is induced, following which they have hallucinatory visions. It has been suggested that the zombie state of the voodoo 'world' is also induced by these powerful alkaloids. Beware – the peripheral effects and hallucinations can last for several days.

# EUPHORBIA CHARACIAS, EUPHORBIA MILII, EUPHORBIA PEPLUS

*Euphorbia characias* 'Silver Swan'

**Euphorbia characias** L. Euphorbiaceae. Distribution: Mediterranean.

**Euphorbia milii** Des Moul. Euphorbiaceae. Crown of Thorns. Distribution: Madagascar.

**Euphorbia peplus** L. Euphorbiaceae. Distribution: Europe, temperate Asia.

here are 2000 species of *Euphorbia* around the world, with about half a dozen to be found wild in Britain. They are amongst the most poisonous of our native flora. The plant is named for Euphorbus (c. 10BCE–20CE), the Greek physician to the Berber King Juba II (c. 50BCE–23CE) of Numidia, North Africa. The word 'spurge' is derived from the French word for purgation as their sap is a violent purgative.[53]

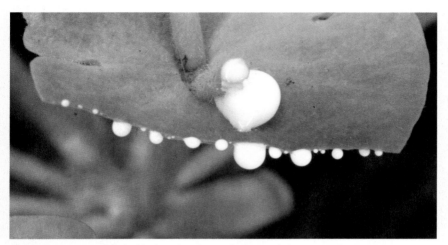

ABOVE: Corrosive sap of *Euphorbia characias* subsp. *wulfenii* – typical of the spurge family
OPPOSITE: Flowers of *Euphorbia characias* subsp. *wulfenii*

Tropical spurges tend to be spiny and cactus-like; those from temperate climes are soft herbaceous plants. They all have a corrosive white latex-like sap and in Europe this has been used as a folk remedy to treat warts – in Germany it is called Wortwurt. Its corrosive effects are due to the terpenes in the sap. One of the Garden Fellows tried it as a child and reports that it made the warts scabby, but did not remove them.

Dioscorides, writing on *Euphorbia characias* (Mediterranean Spurge), advises that two obols (just over one gram) of the sap made into pills caused vomiting and diarrhoea. He recognised the corrosive effect of the sap and advised coating oneself with oil or suet when extracting the sap in case it splashed onto the skin, and coating the pills with wax to avoid the sap burning the throat. He used it for toothache, applied to the tooth; as a depilatory; for treating warts, cutaneous papillomas (skin tags), cancers, gangrene and

fistulas. In North Africa, the sap (probably dried) was administered inside a fig for the reason noted by Dioscorides, a technique used today, rather more subtly, with 'enteric coated' medications. It can cause skin allergies and the smoke from burning it is toxic.

Gerard (1633) apparently did not know that the sap of *Euphorbia* was corrosive for he writes: 'I took but one drop of it into my mouth; which nevertheless did so inflame and swell in my throat that I hardly escaped with my life.'

A grandson (Freddie) of one of the Garden Fellows attended a 'Forest School' – boy scouts without the sing-songs – and the ex-army instructor advised him and other the eight-year-olds that edible foods could be identified by just pressing them with one's lips. Freddie tried this on Dog's Mercury, (*Mercurialis perennis*), an English woodland plant which carpets the ground through spring and summer.

Common spurge, *Euphorbia peplus*, used for skin cancers

**We cultivate *E. peplus* in the wild flowerbed under the Hippocratic plane tree in the College lawn. It appears without aid from the gardeners (as it does in every garden) after the winter aconites have died down. Most people regard it as a weed and remove it; we put a label on it.**

It too is a member of the Euphorbiaceae and one of our most poisonous plants. Even though he did not bite into it he experienced much the same symptoms as Gerard. His mother (and grandfather) were not amused.

*Euphorbia milii* is one of the tropical spurges, with fierce, cactus-like spines and pretty, long-lasting, red flowers. It is grown as a house plant. The sap is the source of a potential anti-leukaemic chemical, lasiodoplin, which is not in clinical use. It is used in drainage ditches to kill the snails which carry the parasitic trematode which causes fasciolaris. It does not kill the fish, although sap from other euphorbias is toxic to them. It was named after Baron Pierre Barnard Milius, the Governor of Mauritius (1819–1821).

Recent studies have shown that the sap of Common Spurge, *E. peplus*, is effective against basal cell carcinomas and other skin cancers.[60] Topical Ingenol mebutate gel, derived from this plant, is proving a useful addition to other therapies. It has been through the stage of being the new 'wonder drug', but a dermatologist Fellow writes: 'I must say that from what I have seen of the clinical effects of Ingenol when applied to a simple actinic keratosis on the face of an elderly patient leading a quiet life in Aldeburgh that it comes very close to breaking my golden rule of "not making the treatment worse than the disease".' We cultivate *E. peplus* in the wild flowerbed under the Hippocratic plane tree in the College lawn. It appears without aid from the gardeners (as it does in every garden) after the winter aconites have died down. Most people regard it as a weed and remove it; we put a label on it.

OPPOSITE: *Euphorbia milii*: the sap kills the mollusc hosts to parasitic trematodes

# HERBAL MEDICINES

Most of the world uses some herbal medicines. Ninety per cent of the plants in the Garden are not used in conventional medicine today, but were used by our medical predecessors or, at some time, somewhere, or now, in what has become known as alternative medicine. We can only choose a few. Some are registered as Traditional Herbal Medicines in the UK; no proof of efficacy is required, only evidence of use by herbalists over a number of years and some indication of the absence of serious toxicity. Others, which have been granted a Marketing Authorisation licence, have been shown, scientifically, to be effective. Patient Information Leaflets, agreed packaging and manufacturing criteria are required, making both types a much more regulated product. They can be sold 'over the counter' without prescription. Others – like *Aristolochia*, previously discussed – are banned substances, but any person who sets up as a herbalist can otherwise dispense what they like to a patient on a face-to-face interview. Some are available on prescription.

**Ninety per cent of the plants in the Garden are not used in conventional medicine today, but were used by our medical predecessors or, at some time, somewhere, or now, in what has become known as alternative medicine.**

One of the difficulties about herbal medicines is the tendency (and it is not just herbalists who do this) for authors to state 'used by the ancients for thousands of years' without source literature. The other is trying to identify what plant was meant by any given name. A 'Spurge', or 'Euphorbia', could be any of 2000 different species and the gradual use of binomials, e.g. Common Spurge, *Euphorbia peplus,* made an enormous difference to identification. In this section, we will trace the names and uses from different eras and countries of herbal medicines that are now known by their modern nomenclature. Identifying diseases which were treated historically is often impossible: choler was not cholera; scurvy was not vitamin C deficiency; and 'wandering of the mother' was 'hysteria' (whatever that was) due to the uterus wandering about the body. Treatment of fractures, wounds, pain and childbirth; poisons, purgatives and emetics are identifiable. Diseases of the heart were more likely to be emotional than cardiac and the spleen seems to come in for a lot of incrimination although our ancestors would have had no idea of its function.

OPPOSITE: Cone flower, *Echinacea purpurea,* in the North American bed

The Cone Flower, *Echinacea purpurea*, used by Native Americans for coughs and venereal disease, but in modern herbal medicine as an 'immunostimulant'

# ECHINACEA PURPUREA

***Echinacea purpurea*** (L.) Moench. Asteraceae. Cone flower. Distribution: Central and eastern USA.

e include the echinaceas here to compare original, historic uses, modern herbal uses and the use approved by the MHRA.[48]

Austin (2004) recorded the oral tradition of medicinal plant usage by indigenous Native Americans and found that the roots of *Echinacea purpurea* were chewed or used as a tincture for coughs by the Choctaw. Combined with *Rhus typhina* it was used to treat venereal disease by the Delaware. On the whole it was little used by Native Americans, who used *E. angustifolia* very widely, regarding it as a panacea and magical herb. This and *E. pallida* were used to treat snake bite, spider bite, cancer, toothache, burns, sores, wounds, flu and colds.

*Echinacea purpurea* is now used in herbal medicine as an 'immunostimulant'. *Potter's Herbal Cyclopaedia* lists two dozen chemicals found in *Echinacea pallida, E. angustifolia* and *E. purpurea* including caffeic acid conjugates; unsaturated isobutyl amides; polysaccharides; essential oils; derivatives of labdane; and linoleic acid, rutin, vanillin; and the alkaloids tussilagine and isotussilagine.[90] These chemicals are not present in all *Echinacea* species and none of them have been shown to be useful medicines. Taking drops

Amongst the visitors to the Garden, the consensus is that Echinacea is taken throughout the winter to ward off colds or taken at the onset of a cold to shorten the duration. It works for some and not for others.

of a tincture or as tablets orally, *Echinacea* is recommended by herbalists as being antiviral, antibacterial, for healing wounds and as an alterative (a medicine to restore health). Specifically it is used for skin diseases, boils, carbuncles and *septicaemia* [author's italics], tonsillitis and pharyngitis. But 'the most important action of *Echinacea* is probably its ability to stimulate the immune system … (by) stimulation of phagocytosis'. The latter concept of phagocytes (white blood cells) ingesting bacteria, was proposed by Sir Almroth Wright and immortalised by George Bernard Shaw in *The Doctor's Dilemma* more than a century ago.[94] The ability of extracts of *Echinacea*, 'especially the polysaccharide fraction', to 'activate macrophages, causing an increase in secretion of free radicals and interleukin I' as 'possibly explaining its activity against infections and in some anti-tumour systems' are postulates that are not accepted by modern-day physicians. Potter states that it is safe to take in pregnancy, but no traditional herbal medicine has MHRA approval for this.[48]

Thirty-two different products containing '*Echinacea purpurea* dry extract' are registered in the UK. There are another two dozen containing root extracts, including a Duchy brand from Prince Charles' company. Six products containing *E. angustifolia* and one containing *E. pallida* are also listed. Many will be the same compound medicine under a different brand name and many contain other ingredients, herbal and inorganic. Registration is granted on the basis of traditional use, 'to relieve the symptoms of the common cold and influenza type infections' and not from clinical trials. Additionally, 'There is no requirement under the Traditional Herbal Registration scheme to prove scientifically that the product works.' Side effects range from anaphylactic shock to reduced white cells and platelets with increased infections, and it may trigger autoimmune disorders. Consequently the MHRA recommends that it should not be used for longer than eight weeks.[48]

Amongst the visitors to the Garden, the consensus is that Echinacea is taken throughout the winter to ward off colds or taken at the onset of a cold to shorten the duration. It works for some and not for others. The discrepancy between the MHRA's recommendations and some in *Potter's Herbal Cyclopaedia* – e.g. to treat septicaemia – is extremely worrying. The additives in the manufactured products add extra side effects. Whether one believes that *Echinacea purpurea* is a placebo or a useful medicine, the one consistent indication – from the Choctaw in North America to *Potter's Herbal* and the MHRA – is for treating coughs. In the origins of the herbal medicine tradition in North America, *E. pallida* and *E. angustifolia* were valued more.

# SENNA CORYMBOSA

**Senna corymbosa** (Lam.) H.S. Irwin & Barneby. Caesalpinaceae. Previously in the genus *Cassia*. Senna. Distribution: Argentina (other species from Europe).

rom midsummer until the frosts of winter this beautiful shrub flowers continuously under the olive tree on the College lawn. It is the source of one of the best known of all herbal medicines – Senokot (and Senna pods and Senna tea made from the dried leaves). It is included because, despite the good work of the MHRA, Patient Information Leaflets can still be produced without adequate guidance or warnings of dangerous side effects.[48]

It was introduced to European medicine (as *Senna alexandrina* from Egypt) by the Arabian Mesue (c. 800CE, physician to Caliph Haroun-al-Raschid, of the *Arabian Nights*) and Serapion (eleventh century). Every part of the plant contains anthraquinones which, if taken internally, act as a powerful laxative to treat constipation. Gerard (1633) notes 'it is a singular purging medicine' and includes over a page on its uses. When used over a long period the ganglion cells in the large bowel may be damaged, leaving a permanently dilated large bowel that never functions properly again, although this is disputed.[50,66] This is a plant which causes the condition it treats to become permanent. Additionally, the lining of the bowel turns black, a condition called *melanosis coli*, due to the accumulation of pigment-laden macrophages. Serum potassium levels may fall, resulting in cardiac irregularities and sometimes death. Coma, neuropathy and reversible hepatotoxicity have also been reported.

Lyte (1578) recommends Senna strongly for depression. It is advertised on television: the actress involved is seen to be bloated and depressed until she takes a Senna product, after which she is happy, bouncing about with her

ABOVE: *Senna corymbosa*
OPPOSITE: Flowers of *Senna corymbosa*. All parts of the plant contain a powerful purgative

girlfriends. Hippocrates would have attributed this antidepressant effect to the plant's ability to purge her of the black melancholic humour present in her bowel motions.

Senna leaf products are registered by the MHRA 'for the short term relief of occasional constipation, based on traditional use only', but also have a Marketing Authorisation licence which indicates that effectiveness and safety are proven. The Patient Information Leaflet makes no mention of 'for the short term relief of occasional constipation', merely saying 'If you need to take Senna every day … consult your doctor'. There is no mention of any of the side effects noted above and it is available in packs of up to 1000 tablets. At two tablets a day for sixteen months this would appear to be quite sufficient to do irreparable damage.

# VITEX AGNUS-CASTUS

**Vitex agnus-castus** L. Lamiaceae. Chaste Tree, Monk's Pepper. Distribution: Mediterranean and central Asia.

 eaves, flowers and berries of this plant may all be consumed as a decoction, tincture, syrup or elixir or simply eaten straight off the plant as a medicinal food. The name comes from the Greek *agonos*, meaning 'no progeny' i.e. 'infertile', and later *agnos*, meaning 'pure, chaste'. When Latinised to *Agnus* – meaning 'lamb' – its original meaning was lost. *Castus*, however, is Latin for 'chaste' and, as Cole (1657) has pointed out, to call a plant 'chaste-chaste' is a tautology. The name *Vitex* was first used by Pliny and may be derived from 'vitilis', Latin for 'pliant', and refer to the use of the wiry branches for making baskets. The ability of *Vitex agnus-castus* to stimulate lactation and reduce libido, first reported two millennia ago, is now attributed to its ability to raise prolactin levels, hence the name Chaste Tree. In Classical Greece (ca. 600BCE–600CE) at the feast of the Thesmophoria, in honour of Demeter and Persephone, married women used to leave their husbands and live together for a while, practising sexual abstinence. Pliny reports of *V. agnus-castus* that 'they made their pallets and beds with the leaves thereof, to coole the heat of lust and to keep themselves chast(e) for the time'. He also advises that it induces menstruation and that it has 'this speciall property besides, to breed good store of milk in milch nurses [women who provided breast milk for other people's babies]'. Dioscorides agrees: 'It bringeth down the milke, and expels the menstrua … it destroys generation [i.e. prevents sexual activity]'. He also advised that a traveller carrying a branch of the tree would experience no fatigue – a myth which was reprinted for nearly 1800 years.

Bartholemeus Anglicus wrote in 1240 in *De Proprietabis rerum* that women ate the dried fruits when it was necessary to remain celibate ('*quando … necessario continentiam observare*') (Anglicus, 1492) and in John Trevisa's English translation 'the herbe agnus-castus … for wyth smel and vse it maketh men chaste as a lombe [lamb]'.

OPPOSITE: The Chaste tree, *Vitex agnus-castus*

The Chaste tree, *Vitex agnus-castus*, an anaphrodisiac

It is in the College's *Pharmacopoeia Londinensis* (1618), its use given by Culpeper (1649) as: 'The leaves … consume the seed [? cause impotence], cause Chastity being only born about one [viz. carried], dissolves swelling of the Cods [testicles] being applied to them'. The concept that medicinal properties can be transmuted into the body still continues in this era and, while none of our Garden visitors have been seen wearing copper bracelets for rheumatism, we have had one man who had carried a wine cork in his pocket for over twenty years to prevent him getting cramp. He reported that it worked and he had never had cramp since carrying it.

Parkinson (1640) writes that the seed of *V. agnus-castus* is so hot that it causes headaches, but less so if dried and fried. If dried and fried further 'it restraineth also the instigations to venery'. He notes a paradox from Galen, who in one place says it reduces desire and in another says it increases it. More recently, this plant has been called Monk's Pepper on the basis that it was used as anti-libido medicine by monks to aid their attempts to remain chaste, the seeds being ground up and sprinkled on their food. This name is derived from the German 'Mönchspfeffer', but the date of introduction is obscure; this was not a German name for it pre-1750 and no pre-1900 source for it being used by monks has been found. However, as the raw seed is very 'hot' and like pepper, it would have been expected to *stimulate* lust. One can speculate that the seeds were cooked for a long time, as Parkinson (above) has noted.

Modern evidence for *V. agnus-castus* being aphrodisiac and/or anaphrodisiac is weak. If it raises prolactin, this will cause suppression of sexual desire, for prolactin levels increase after sexual activity and counteract the effect of dopamine, which is responsible for sexual arousal. Raised prolactin levels are thought to cause the male sexual refractory period. The plasma level of prolactin can be an indicator for the amount of sexual satisfaction and relaxation. Unusually high amounts, such as those occurring with certain pituitary tumours, are suspected to be responsible for impotence and loss of libido. Merz *et al* found that men treated with high doses of *Vitex agnus-castus* extract experienced a slight reduction of prolactin levels, whereas lower doses caused a slight increase compared with placebo.[47] Such a decrease in prolactin levels would lead to an increase in desire. However, the amount of sexual activity engaged in during the study would have had a significant effect on the findings and no comment is made about the effects on libido.

> More recently, this plant has been called Monk's Pepper on the basis that it was used as anti-libido medicine by monks to aid their attempts to remain chaste, the seeds being ground up and sprinkled on their food.

Raised prolactin levels can cause breast engorgement premenstrually and a contrary view has been made that extracts of *V. agnus-castus* can *reduce* prolactin levels and so alleviate the condition. A review of its health benefits in twelve randomised clinical trials in premenstrual syndromes suggested that it was beneficial, but that further study was required.[84]

It is registered for use by the UK MHRA to help relieve premenstrual symptoms such as irritability, mood swings, breast tenderness, bloating and menstrual cramps, based on traditional use only.[48]

# PLANTS FOR TREATING CANCER

The toxic chemicals that plants have produced during the 370 million years of their existence and evolution to deter predators run into millions, so the ability of some of them to produce chemicals that stop cell division should not be surprising. Chance, with selection driven by evolutionary pressures, is a powerful combination. Pharmaceutical science can convert these chemicals into specific anti-cancer drugs and, in a similar process to evolution, drugs which are successful come into widespread use and form the basis of even more successful drugs. Many have been found by serendipity in vast phyto-screening programmes. Here we describe two genera and our first, *Veratrum*, includes a milestone in the care of women in pregnancy, discovered long before the oncologic potential of its sister species was known.

## VERATRUM ALBUM

**Veratrum album** L. Melanthiaceae. White hellebore, called 'Elleborus Albus' in the *Pharmacopoeia Londinensis* (1618). Distribution: Europe, North Africa, northern Asia.

 ows do not eat *Veratrum* species in the Swiss alpine meadows, and human poisoning with it cause vomiting and fainting. Sheep in California are not so bright, which has led to the discovery of potential new cancer therapies.

Historically, *Veratrum album* (and *V. nigrum*) have been recognised as violent poisons. Pliny writes at length (2500 words) of the dangers of *Veratrum* and the superstitions surrounding it, and notes that a goat which had eaten it was violently purged. The goat's milk was given to the daughters of King Praetus who were thus 'cured of their furious melancholy and brought again to their right wits'. This might inspire a search for antipsychotic activity in this most interesting and poisonous plant. In the College Garden we grow *Veratrum album, Veratrum album* var. *flavum, Veratrum nigrum* and *Veratrum californicum*. We do not grow *Veratrum viride* but a chemical called veratrum is present in all of them.

In the 1850s, extracts of *Veratrum album* were found to reduce the heart's action and slow the pulse. Bentley (1861) wrote:

OPPOSITE: The medicine from this plant, *Veratrum nigrum*, saved women with eclampsia

*Veratrum ...The rhizomes of* V. album *are commonly known as White Hellebore roots. They contain the alkaloid Veratria, and another alkaloid named Jervin. White Hellebore is a narcotico-acrid poison. ... The rhizome of* V. viride, *Green Hellebore is now much employed in the United States ... as an arterial sedative.*

This action as an aterial sedative was later shown to be a reflex action, the Bezold-Jarisch reflex, whereby receptors in the great vessels are stimulated, increasing vagal output from the medulla causing bradycardia, vasodilatation and also vomiting.[7, 33]

In 1859 *Veratrum*, mistakenly believed to be an anticonvulsant, was used orally in a woman who was having convulsions due to eclampsia, a specific condition occurring in pregnancy due to high blood pressure. Dr Paul DeLacy Baker in Alabama treated her with drops of a tincture of *V. viride* and she recovered.[15] By 1947 death rates at the Boston Lying-In Hospital from eclampsia had been reduced from 30% to 5% by the use of *Veratrum*.[31] It was subsequently used as the treatment of first choice for eclampsia. When blood pressure monitoring became possible, it was realised that extracts of *Veratrum* worked by reducing the high blood pressure rather than as an anticonvulsant. Nevertheless vomiting and a very narrow therapeutic window were always problems and currently the agent of choice for both treatment and prophylaxis is intravenous magnesium sulphate.[63,75]

As a herbal medicine *Veratrum* is regulated as a prescription-only drug by the MHRA.[79]

# VERATRUM CALIFORNICUM

**Veratrum californicum** L. Melanthiaceae. California False hellebore. Distribution: North America.

 further use of *Veratrum* species was developed when it was noted that *V. californicum* and (other species) if eaten by sheep, resulted in foetal malformations, in particular lambs with only one eye. The chemical in the plant responsible for the cyclops defect, cyclopamine, was found to act on certain genetic pathways controlling stem cell division and regulation of the development of bilateral symmetry in the embryo. Synthetic analogues have been developed which act on what have come to be called the 'hedgehog signalling pathways' in stem cell division. These 'hedgehog inhibitors', saridegib, erismodegib and vismodegib, are being introduced into medicine for the treatment of various cancers such as chondrosarcoma, myelofibrosis and advanced basal cell carcinoma.[12] This was serendipity for us, less fortunate for the sheep.

The European Yew, *Taxus baccata*, revolutionised the treatment of breast cancer

**The chemistry of taxol was complex and novel so identification took several years ... It showed particular promise against cells from certain solid tumours which were otherwise very difficult to treat.**

# TAXUS BACCATA

***Taxus baccata*** L. Taxaceae. European Yew. Distribution: Western, central and southern Europe, northwest Africa, northern Iran and southwest Asia.

ew trees have long had a gloomy reputation as being poisonous and associated with graves and death as they are commonly grown in churchyards. They may be there because Christian churches were built on the sites of yew tree groves, which were sacred in pagan beliefs, and the yew trees were there before the churches. Yew has now become an important source of life in the face of death as the basis of a very successful group of anti-cancer drugs – the taxanes, derived from naturally occurring taxines.[23]

The yew tree has a well-proven reputation as being highly toxic due mainly to taxine alkaloids, present in highest concentration in the seeds and with a lower level in the needles. They both contain ephedrine and the cyanogenic glycoside taxiphyllin. The taxines cause cardiac dysfunction and hypotension through calcium channel blockade, with cardiac damage and arrest, vomiting and confusion.[91] The poisonous alkaloids persist in the dried plant. The red flesh of the berry (the aril) is not toxic. Severe toxicity and even death have followed ingestion of about forty to fifty needles or a tea made from 50–100g of the needles. Farm animals are susceptible, notably horses. Birds are not affected by eating the berries because their beaks and digestive system do not break open the seed, which passes through intact, becoming the principal means of seed dissemination.

In the 1960s, a large screening programme in America identified a potent agent, taxol, in the bark of the Pacific Yew, *Taxus brevifolia*. It was one of only two good leads identified from surveillance of almost 100,000 extracts from 12,000 plant species. The other was irinotecan, an anti-cancer drug from the Chinese tree *Camptotheca acuminata*. The chemistry of taxol was complex and novel so identification took several years, during which extended biological testing showed a unique effect of likely therapeutic value: it stabilised intracellular microtubules and so arrested mitosis and stopped cell proliferation. It showed particular promise against cells from certain solid tumours which were otherwise very difficult to treat with the available chemotherapeutic agents. It was apparent that obtaining a clinically useful and affordable supply of taxol (now paclitaxel) would be a major problem in further clinical work. Continuing to extract it from the bark of the Pacific Yew was impossible because its concentration was low (< 1g per kg bark).

Much new chemistry and clever pharmaceutics were needed, taking more than ten years and the involvement of a major pharmaceutical firm, before sufficient drug was available for the formal clinical studies that showed paclitaxel to be of unique value in the treatment of breast and ovarian cancers. It was finally approved in 1993 but only after a brand new semisynthetic route had been discovered and developed into an industrially workable process. In the final manufacturing process 10-deacetylbaccatin was extracted from the needles of the much more plentiful European Yew, *T. baccata,* followed by a short sequence of reactions with a reasonable yield to produce paclitaxel. Subsequently, chemical and industrial developments have led to commercial production in industrial fermenters, containing a cell line from the European Yew and an endophytic

fungus, *Penicillium raistrickii*.[44] Once an acceptable, although still awkward, solvent had been found (Cremophor, derived from *Ricinus communis* (see page 13) the drug was rapidly adopted throughout the world. It became the first anti-cancer drug to achieve US $1 billion sales in a year as its therapeutic value became accepted and new uses were found. A close analogue, docetaxel, was synthesised and approved in 1998. Taxanes are the mainstays of chemotherapy of cancers of the ovary and pancreas and are also widely used to treat stomach, lung and breast tumours. More recently, they have been used to stop the cells lining the coronary arteries from growing into and blocking stents inserted to improve coronary artery blood flow.[71]

Dioscorides says the tree is so poisonous that those who sit or sleep under it die. Pliny's total contribution is that the fumes and smoke of Yew trees kill mice and rats. Lobel (1576) says the word 'toxic' is derived from '*Taxus*' and that it was lethal and used to poison arrows. He attributes the story of the death of those who sleep under it to Plutarch (46–120CE). In the sixteenth and seventeenth centuries Parkinson, Culpeper, Lyte and Matthiolus (1586) all say it is dangerous; only Gerard (1633) says that he has eaten the berries and slept under the tree without harm, but none of them recommend it for any medicinal use. It is not mentioned in the eighteenth century by Bergius (1782), Murray (1776) or Woodville (1792) and it is not till the nineteenth century that we find uses creeping in – transiently, as a *Digitalis* substitute – and for inducing menstruation and as a sedative and antispasmodic.

From the 1920s onwards ephedrine, as a purified extract from E. sinica ... came into increasing use as a bronchodilator in asthma.

# PLANTS AS SOURCES OF MODERN MEDICINES

We grow about fifty plants in the Garden which were the original sources of modern medicines, some of which we have already discussed. However, ephedrine, which progressed from a treatment for asthma to being the source of an illegal 'high'; dimethylbiguanide (Metformin) for Type 2 diabetes; sodium valproate for epilepsy and oseltamivir (Tamiflu) for bird flu and swine flu, seem worthy of inclusion.

## EPHEDRA SINICA, EPHEDRA GERARDIANA

**Ephedra sinica** Stapf. Ephedraceae. Ma Huang; Mormon, Brigham or Whorehouse Tea. Distribution: Temperate Asia, China.

**Ephedra gerardiana** Stapf. Ephedraceae. Indian Jointfir; Pakistani Ephedra. Distribution: Afghanistan, China, India.

*Ephedra sinica*, the source of the chemical ephedrine

 eferences in Western literature as far back as Dioscorides to plants called *Tithymalus* are likely to have been *E. fragilis* var. *graeca*. In China and India plants of this type have been mentioned in classical accounts, for religious as well as medical purposes, for at least 5000 years.[11] *Ephedra* plants are found in the Ebers Papyrus, dated 1550BCE, from Egypt. Preparations of these plants have long been used in southeastern Asia to treat melancholia, to enhance alertness and to help breathing in various chest diseases. In the West in the latter part of the nineteenth century extracts were used as mydriatics to dilate the pupil. From the 1920s onwards ephedrine, as a

OPPOSITE: Fruits of *Ephedra sinica*, a primitive flowering plant

*Ephedra gerardiana* var. *sikkimensis*

purified extract from *E. sinica* and later as the pure synthetic alkaloid, came into increasing use as a bronchodilator in asthma, as a stimulant to produce weight loss (often combined in 'Stacks' with aspirin and caffeine) and to improve exercise performance. Native Americans in North America had long drunk tea made from the stems of local species (such as *E. antisyphilitica* and *E. viridis*) to treat syphilis and backache, regulate menstruation and topically to treat snake bite and wounds (USDA). An unfounded belief in its prophylactic and curative antisyphilitic activity accounts for the popular name of 'Whorehouse (or Miscarriage) Tea', as it was served in the waiting areas of bordellos in Nevada and California. Mormons drank it because it did not contain the caffeine forbidden by their religion, although there are other related stimulant chemicals in the species which they used in Utah.[9]

*Ephedra gerardiana* and its varieties are named after the Gerard family of Scottish soldiers and scientists, including Dr James Gilbert Gerard (1793–1835), who explored and travelled widely in the British Army in India in the early nineteenth century and collected many plants in Nepal and Afghanistan. The principal sources of *Ephedra* plant products remain China (annual exports up to 30,000 tons) and India, but much larger quantities of ephedrine are now made synthetically in Germany.[29]

The pharmacological activities of the Ephedraceae are due to their content of alkaloids, the best known being ephedrine and its diastereoisomer, pseudoephedrine, which have been found in variable concentrations in most species.[11, 9] Ephedrine and pseudoephedrine are relatively non-selective agonists at pre- and postsynaptic β-adrenoreceptors. They may have variable actions on the α-receptors and they enhance the activity of epinephrine released from sympathetic nerve endings by blocking its reuptake.[1, 19, 42] Pseudoephedrine is less active on the heart and blood pressure.

The use of ephedrine for asthma was discontinued when the selective bronchodilators became available in the 1970s. The side effects of agitation and tachycardia were always unwelcome. Pseudoephedrine has been used as a local decongestant ('Benylin' and 'Sudafed' in over-the-counter medicines) for decades, both systemically and as a nasal application, as it constricts the blood vessels in the nasal mucosa. It is also given with local anaesthetics to cause vasoconstriction and so increase the length of time that lignocaine remains in the tissues. Excessive doses of the alkaloids can raise the blood pressure, produce cardiac disorders, agitation and even seizures and death. Official restrictions have been applied because of the health risks of unrestricted use of herbal *Ephedra* products, especially their abuse to counter obesity.[4,48,64] Athletes in competitive sports are not allowed to take *Ephedra*/ephedrine. Legal controls have been applied to ephedrine itself as a precursor in the backstreet manufacture of illegal 'highs', such as methamphetamine, methcathinone and Ecstasy (3,4-methylenedioxy-methamphetamine). The latter is estimated to be used by up to 28 million people worldwide.[82]

Flowers of *Ephedra gerardiana* var. *sikkimensis*

# GALEGA OFFICINALIS

**Galega officinalis** L. Papilionaceae (or Fabaceae). Goat's Rue, French lilac, Holy Hay, Italian fitch, *Ruta capraria*, Lavanése, Spanish sanfoin, false indigo or professor-weed. Distribution: Western Asia, although naturalised elsewhere including southern Europe.

 *alega officinalis* is the original source of the biguanides – Phenformin and Metformin – used for Type 2 diabetes. This account will start with its etymology and its alleged historic uses.

It is possible that it was known as *Galega* from the beginning of the sixteenth century; the common name of 'Goat's Rue' arises from its Latin name of *Ruta capraria,* used since the early years of the College. Matthiolus (1554), while discussing Rue (*Ruta graveolens*), writes that there is another species of Rue, more recently known as *Capraria* (Latin for a female goatherd) whose real name is *Galega*. His description fits that of *G. officinalis* and in his *De Plantis Epitome* (1586) he illustrates it with a woodcut, under *Galega sive* [or] *Ruta capraria*. *Ruta* is Latin for anything dug from the ground for household use, including gravel, stones and presumably plants. Its first use in diabetes has been attributed to Culpeper, but in fact all Culpeper has to say about diabetes in 1649 is 'A sheep or Goats bladder being burnt and the ashes given inwardly, helps the *Diabetes* or continual pissing'.[5] What he has to say about *Galega* is: '*Galega*. Goat's Rue: … resists poyson, kills worms, helps the falling sickness [epilepsy], resisteth the pestilence', which is taken from Matthiolus (above). Neither does he write in any of his later books that *Galega* or *Ruta graveolens* were used for diabetes, despite numerous claims by modern authors that he does. In *The Practice of Physick* (Riverius, Culpeper & Cole, 1661) over thirty plants are recommended as cures for diabetes and none of them is *Galega* or *Ruta graveolens*.

GALEGA SIVE RVTA CAPRARIA.

ABOVE: Galega officinalis, Goat's Rue, as Galega sive Ruta caprariae from Matthiolus's *De Plantis Epitome* (1586)
OPPOSITE: *Galega officinalis*, source of Metformin for diabetes

There is a belief that G. *officinalis* is a galactogogue (stimulates milk production) in farm animals (Mori et al, 1985), so its common name relates to its being eaten by goats to increase milk production.[41] This is a fiction. It is regarded as a noxious weed in North America, causing pulmonary oedema, hypotension, paralysis and death in cattle, so even the concept of it being an animal galactogogue seems unlikely. Mrs Grieve's *Modern Herbal* (1931) says that the leaves when crushed give off a disagreeable odour (as do goats) and taste bitter. It is clear that she had not tried this as the plant in the College tastes of pea pods and the leaves are odourless when crushed.

The belief that it was used historically as a galactogogue and for diabetes is so engrained in the literature that a review is required. Statements such as the one below deserve to be refuted:

> **A prime example of a plant treatment that has provided a source of such drug templates is G. officinalis *(galega, Goat's rue, French lilac).* Galega *is well known for its hypoglycaemic action and has been used in Europe for the treatment of diabetes mellitus since medieval times [i.e. pre-1500]. (Watson and Preedy, 2008)*[88]**

A literature search revealed the following: *Galega officinalis* (in any of its synonyms) is not mentioned in the English translations of Dioscorides by Goodyear in 1633 (Gunther, 1959) or Beck, 2005; nor is it in Fuchs, 1542 and 1551; Ruel, 1543; Cordus, 1546; Dodoens, 1554; or Fernelius, 1593. It is in L'Escluse, 1557; Matthiolus, 1569 and 1586; Pena

and Lobel, 1570; Lobel, 1576; Lyte, 1578; Dodoens, 1583; *Pharmacopoeia Londinensis* of 1618; Gerard, 1633; Parkinson, 1640; Culpeper, 1649 and 1650 but not his subsequent publications Coles, 1657; Bauhin, 1680; and James, 1752. None of them make any mention of its use as a galactogogue or for treating diabetes, only for palpitations, melancholy, snake bite, all infections with skin spots from measles to plague, intestinal worms, epilepsy in children and ulcers. Gerard adds that the seeds, fed to chickens, increase egg production. By 1718, it was decried as being 'a useless ingredient in the *milk water*' (which may refer to a galactogogue) and most of its reputed medicinal properties mere fables (Quincy, 1718).

*Galega* is given in the Italian translation of Lemerey (1719–20) as an ingredient of *Aqua Vitae Mulierum* (Aqua Vita of Women) for strengthening the viscera, in particular the uterus, and to induce the menses and sweating. However, the English version (Hamel, 1700) has translated *Galega* as *Galangal* which was a term for a plant in the ginger family, which seems more likely. It was in the College's *Pharmacopoeia* of 1724 (as *Ruta capraria*). It is not in Murray's *Apparatus Medicaminum* (1776–92) or Woodville (1790), nor can we find it in nineteenth century pharmaceutical literature. Nowhere was it used for diabetes.

Contemporary use of *Galega officinalis* as a galactogogue in humans is not encouraged by The Academy of Breastfeeding Medicine Protocol Committee; there are no adequate clinical trials confirming its efficacy in this respect and there are reports of breast-feeding

Contemporary use of *Galega officinalis* as a galactogogue in humans is not encouraged by The Academy of Breastfeeding Medicine Protocol Committee; there are no adequate clinical trials confirming its efficacy.

neonates becoming ill as a result of their mothers drinking more than two litres a day of a herbal tea containing Goat's Rue and other alleged galactogogues.[2] It does not have a licence for any use under the UK Traditional Herbal Medicine Registration scheme.

The prospect of better management for diabetes arose in the early part of the twentieth century when it was shown that guanidine from *Galega officinalis* could improve the symptoms of late onset (Type 2) diabetes mellitus, even though it was too toxic for human use.[70,87] Simonnet and Tanret (1927) identified another alkaloid from *G. officinalis*, galegine, (isoamylene guanidine) that was less toxic.[65,51] However, clinical trials in the 1920s and 1930s in patients with diabetes were unsuccessful.[6,93] Two further synthetic diguanides, decamethylene diguanide (Synthalin A) and dodecamethylene diguanide (Synthalin B), were used clinically for diabetes in the 1920s. Concern about toxicity and lack of effect by comparison with insulin led to discontinuation of the Synthalins. Jean Sterne (1909–1997), a French diabetologist, also conducted studies with galegine. In 1956, at the Hôpital Laennec in Paris he successfully explored the anti-diabetic properties of the related biguanides, including dimethylbiguanide (Metformin), which has made such a huge impact on the treatment of diabetes.[69]

Guanidine, the diguanides and the biguanides (Phenformin and Metformin) act by decreasing insulin resistance by increasing glucose uptake by cells and by suppressing glucose production in the liver (hepatic gluconeogenesis).[14] These actions are likely to be mediated at least in part by the activation of a 5' AMP-activated protein kinase (AMPK), an enzyme that plays an important role in insulin signalling. Metformin, introduced to the United Kingdom in 1958, is now believed to be the most widely prescribed anti-diabetic drug in the world. It is the mainstay in the treatment of gestational diabetes (which is a major risk factor for very large babies) and the Metabolic Syndrome (obesity, diabetes, hyperlipidaemia, vascular disease) where it is used to reverse the associated polycystic ovaries and infertility.

# VALERIANA OFFICINALIS

**Valeriana officinalis** L. Valerianaceae. *Valerianus, Phu, Nardus sylvestris*, Setwal, Zedoarium. Distribution: Europe.

 From this plant a powerful and effective treatment for epilepsy, sodium valproate, has been derived. Its use in herbal medicine over 2000 years is slight, but there are references that

indicate that it was used for anxiety and, from the end of the sixteenth century, for epilepsy.

Pliny says it: '… is excellent for the rising of the Mother [=uterus], which threateneth suffocation; for the pains of the breast and pleurisy'. This curious phrase 'rising/suffocation of the mother' refers to a belief that breathlessness and choking were due to the wandering uterus, in the same way that a large pregnant uterus might cause similar symptoms. The concept of *Valeriana* being good for anxiety may have arisen from this. Tournefort (1719–1730) recommends it for 'hysteric passion' and violent asthma, which could also be interpreted as being a sedative. Fabio Colonna (1567–1640), writing in 1592 (Colonna, 1744), recommended *Valeriana*

*sylvestris* after an almost endless essay on whether it was the *Nardus* or *Phu* of ancient authors, as a remedy for epilepsy, writing that: '*Epilepsia correoptos liberat* [it frees from the grip of epilepsy]'. Colonna suffered from epilepsy and Woodville (1792) reports that Colonna cured himself with the root of this plant, but suffered a relapse. Woodville lists later authors who have recommended it for epilepsy, but ends with noting that 'our own experience warrants us in saying that it will be seldom found to answer the expectations of the prescriber'. It appears briefly in later pharmacopoeias and its present status is that it is approved by the European Medicines Agency as a traditional herbal medicine for mild anxiety and sleeplessness for up to four weeks.

An argument against it being the *Phu* of Dioscorides is that the latter had flowers bigger than a daffodil (*Narcissus*); the flowers of *V. officinalis* are many and no more than a few millimetres across.

The anti-epileptic medication sodium valproate is made from valproic acid which was synthesised in 1882 as an analogue of valeric acid found in valerian. It is used additionally for neuropathic pain, mania, and for migraine prevention. It is teratogenic, causing autism, facial dysmorphism and low IQs, as well as causing reversible brain damage in infants treated with it. Sadly, effective medicines often have unwanted side effects. We may be dismissive of the ignorance of our predecessors in their medicines and uses, but we still have a long way to go in our understanding of the mode of action of modern treatments, of which sodium valproate is a notable example.

ABOVE and OPPOSITE: *Valerian, Valeriana officinalis*, source of Sodium valproate for treating epilepsy

Tournefort recommends it for 'hysteric passion' and violent asthma, which could also be interpreted as being a sedative.

*Illicium anisatum*, Japanese Star Anise, source of Tamiflu for bird and swine flu

# ILLICIUM ANISATUM, ILLICIUM VERUM

***Illicium anisatum*** L. Illiciaceae. Japanese Star Anise, also *I. religiosum or japonicum; shi-kimi*. Distribution: Japan, China.

***Illicium verum*** Hook.f. Illiciaceae. Chinese Star Anise. Distribution: China.

e grow *Illicium anisatum* (Japanese Star Anise), beside the path near the side entrance to the College, passed every day by the residents from the precinct as they come to lunch. The closely related Chinese Star Anise, *I. verum*, is not cultivated at present. The two species are discussed together as their seed clusters are often confused. *Illicium anisatum* is toxic whereas *I. verum* is the valued culinary spice 'Chinese Star Anise'. Both were used in the manufacture of the anti-influenza drug oseltamivir (Tamiflu), which was widely deployed during recent preparations for an expected H1N1 influenza pandemic.

Choose the right star! The two types of Star Anise are difficult to distinguish by morphology of the seed clusters but this can be done with certainty by chemical analysis to show the presence of carcinogenic safrole and eugenol in *I. anisatum* and their virtual absence from *I. verum*.[35,39,86] The poisonous Japanese species contains powerful neurotoxic sesquiterpene lactones, especially anisatin and close analogues, which act as potent irreversible GABA antagonists.[36,49,54,95] Chinese Star Anise, *I. verum*, has a long history of giving pleasure in the kitchen and of safe medicinal use

Poisoning by tea made from imported Star Anise has been a recurrent problem in the Americas and Europe due to accidental contamination of Chinese Star Anise by the Japanese species.

in Traditional Chinese Medicine. It also contains neurotoxins but they are less potent and are present only in low concentrations.[54] The importation of *I. verum* for food use is strictly controlled to exclude contamination with *I. anisatum*.

The dry, brown, star-shaped seed clusters of *I. anisatum* have been used in Japan in incense, and an essential oil distilled from them has been employed as a liniment rubbed over rheumatic joints.[35] The tree is grown around temples as its smell and toxicity are believed to deter the entry of wild animals. It is toxic to the gastrointestinal tract as well as to the brain.[39] Extracts from the seeds of *I. verum* are used as a topical antiseptic, as a tea to treat colic and other abdominal complaints, and to relieve backache.

In the kitchen, Chinese Star Anise, *I. verum*, in its typical star-shaped clusters of seeds, is valued for its characteristic aniseed- and cardamom-like aroma. Its wide use in many dishes from southeastern Asia is being matched by its growing popularity in the West. The Japanese Star Anise, *I. anisatum*, has a weaker, more cardamom-like aroma; no comment on its taste was found.

Poisoning by tea made from imported Star Anise has been a recurrent problem in the Americas and Europe due to accidental contamination of Chinese Star Anise by the Japanese species.[35,39,49, 57] Infants and some adults given the tea have developed loss of consciousness, seizures and striking, abnormal movements that have lasted for more than twenty-four hours. Many deaths have been reported. The number and severity of the cases and the difficulty of distinguishing contamination of the Chinese Star Anise seed clusters with even a few seeds of the Japanese species led to official bans on the sale of any Star Anise preparations as herbal medicines.

Medical interest in *I. verum* and *I. anisatum* comes from the industrial extraction of shikimic acid from their seedpods for use in the synthesis of the anti-influenza neuraminidase inhibitor Oseltamivir (Tamiflu). Chinese Star Anise grown commercially in southwestern China has been the main source of the drug, although its replacement by industrial synthesis in an engineered strain of *E. coli* is now coming into use.[22] Lower levels of shikimic acid are found in many other plants, too, as an essential step in the biosynthesis of the aromatic amino acids – tryptophan, tyrosine and phenylalanine.

The Garden is open to the public, and guided tours are given by the Garden Fellows – details on the College website.

# BIBLIOGRAPHY

Selected Bibliography. For other references see *Dramatis Personae* page 9 and https://www.rcplondon.ac.uk/medicinalgardenbook

Anglicus, Bartholomeus wrote *De proprietatibus rerum* in 1240, Nuremburg, A. Koberger,1492.

Anglicus, Gilbertus (1180–1250), *Compendium Medicinae*, Lugduni, J. Saccon, 1510.

Apuleius in Hummelberger, G., *De Medicaminibus herbarum*. Commentary on Apuleius (fourth century), chapter 74, Zurich, C. Froschouer, 1537.

ASH Fact Sheet 2014, Smoking statistics, illness and death. www.ash.org.uk Accessed 7/1/15.

Austin, D.F., *Florida Ethnobotany*, Boca Raton, Florida, CRC, 2004.

Bauhin, G., *Histoire des Plantes de l'Europe* Tom 2., Lyon, Jean-Baptiste de Ville, 1680.

Beck, L.Y. (translator), *Pedanius Dioscorides of Anarzarbus de Materia Medica*, New York, Hildesheim, Zurich, Olms-Weidmann, 2005.

Beckman, R., 'Biguanide (Experimenteller Teil)', in *Handbook of experimental pharmacology 29*, Maske, H. (ed.), Berlin, Springer Verlag, 1971.

Bentley, R., *A Manual of Botany*, John Churchill, London, 1861.

Bergius, P.J., *Materia Medica,* Stockholmiae, Petri Hesselberg, 1782.

Blackwell, E., *A Curious Herbal*, London, John Nourse, 1739.

Bock, Hieronymus, *New Kreutterbuch*, Strasburg, Duch Wendel Rihel, 1539.

Coles, W., *Adam in Eden or Nature's Paradise,* London, J. Streater for Nathaniel Brooke, 1657.

Colonna, F. (Columnae, Fabi), *Phytobasanos*, Florentiniae, I.O. Aerr & Typis Petri Caietani Viviani, 1744.

Culpeper, N., *A Physical Directory*, London, Peter Cole, 1649 (second edition 1650).

Dalrymple, D.G., *Artemisia annua, Artemisinin, ACTs & Malaria Control in Africa: Tradition, Science and Public Policy*, Politics and Prose Bookstore, Washington DC, USA, 2012.

Darwin, C., *On the Origin of Species,* London, John Murray, 1859.

Dioscorides, see Gunther, R.T. (1959) and Beck, L.Y. (2005).

Doll, R. and Hill, A.B., 'The mortality of doctors in relation to their smoking habits', *British Medical Journal,* pp. 1451–1455, 1954.

Egenolph, C., *Herbarum, Arborum, Fruticum, Frumentorum* ...Franc. Christian Egenolph, 1562.

Elliott, J., *A complete collection of the medical and philosophical works of John Fothergill with an account of his life; and occasional notes*, London, John Walker, 1781.

Garrod, A.B., *The Essentials of Materia Medica and Therapeutics*, London, Longmans Green & Co, 1886.

Grieve, M., *A Modern Herbal*, London, Jonathan Cape, 1931.

Gunther, R.T., *The Greek Herbal of Dioscorides*, Englished by John Goodyear 1655, edited and first printed 1933, Hafner Publishing Co, New York, 1959.

Hamel, J.B. du, *Pharmacopoeia Lemeriana contracta Lemery's Universal Pharmacopoeia abridg'd*, London, Walter Kettilby (translation of Lemery's *Farmacopoea* q.v.), 1700.

Hamilton, H.C. and Falconer, W., *The Geography of Strabo*, London, George Bell and Sons, 297, 1903. (From Casaubonis, Isaacus, 1620. *Strabonis Rerum Geographicarum Libri XVII.* Lutetiae Parisiorum.)

Hooker, J.D., *Himalayan Journals*, London, John Murray, 1855.

James, R., *Pharmacopoeia Universalis*, London, J. Hodges, 1752.

L'Obel (Lobel), M. de, *Plantarum seu stirpium historia*, Antwerp, Christopher Plantin, 1576.

Lemerey, N., *Farmacopoea Universale*, Venice, Gio: Gabriel Hertz, 1719–20.

Lewis, W., *An Experimental History of the Materia Medica*, London, H. Baldwin, 1761.

Lindley, J., *Flora Medica*, Longman, Orme, Brown, Green & Longmans, 1838.

Linnaeus, C., *Species Plantarum*, Holmiae, Laurentii Salvii, 1753.

Linnaeus, C., *Materia Medica*, Lipsiae et Erlangae, Wolfgangum Waltherum, 1782.

McCrindle, J.W., The *Invasion of India by Alexander the Great as Described by Arrian, Q. Curtius, Diodoros, Plutarch and Justin. …* A . Constable, 1893.

McDonald, I. and Moss-Gibbons, C., *The Royal College of Physicians and its Collections*, London, James & James, 2001.

Minderer, R., *Pharmacopoeia Augustana*, Augsburg, 1613.

Monardes, N.B., translated by Frampton, J., *Joyfull newes out of the newe founde worlde*, London, Willyam Norton, 1577.

Mori, A., Cohen, B.D. and Lowenthal, A. (eds), *Guanidines—historical, biological, biochemical and clinical aspects of the naturally occurring guanidine compounds*, London, Plenum Press, 1985.

Murray, I.A., *Apparatus Medicaminum*, Gottingae, Joann. Christ. Dieterich, 1776.

Occo III, A., *Pharmacopoeia Augustana* (*Enchiridion sive ut vulgo vocant dispensatorium, compositorum medicamentorum, pro Reipub. Augsburgensis Pharmacopoeis*), Augsburg, 1564.(Available as *A Facsimile of the First Edition of the Pharmacopoeia Augustana*, with essays by Theodor Husemann, State Historical Society of Wisconsin, Madison, 1927.)

Pena, P. and Lobel, M., *Stirpium Adversaria Nova*, London, Purfoetii, 1570.

*Pharmacopoe[i]a Londinensis*, London, Edwardus Griffin, Johannis Marriot, May 1618.

*Pharmacopoeia Collegii Regalis Medicorum Londinensis*, London, T. Wood, 1724.

Piso, W., *Historia naturalis & medicae Indiae Occidentalis libri quinque: De arboris, fructibus & herbis medicis, atque alimentariis nascentibus in Brasilia & regionibus vicinis*, Amstelaedami, Ludovicum et Danielem Elzevirios, 201, 1658.

Porta, G.B., *Phytognomica*, Napoli, Horatio Salvianum, 1588.

Quincy, J., *Pharmacopoeia Officinalis & Extemporanea or Compleat English Dispensatory,* London, A. Bell (and others), 1718.

Riverius, L., Culpeper, N. and Cole, A., *The Practice of Physick*, London, Peter Cole and Edward Cole, 1661.

Ruddock, E., *The Homeopathic vade mecum of modern medicine and surgery*, 1867.

Senac, J.-B. de, *Traité de la structure du coeur, de son action, et de ses maladies*, Paris, Jacques Vincent, 1749.

Sloane, Sir Hans, *A Voyage to the Islands Madera, Barbados, Nieves, S Christophers and Jamaica … with the natural history of the … last of those islands*, London, for the Author, 1707.

Talbor, Sir R., *Pyretologia: a Rational Account of the Cause and Cures of Agues,* London, R. Robinson, 1672.

Tournefort, J.P., *Compleat Herbal,* London, R. Bonwicke et al., 1719–30.

Turner, W., *A New Herball,* London, Steven Mierdman, 1551.

Urdang, G., Hollister Pharmaceutical Library Number Two, 1944. Wisconsin Historical Society, 1943; containing 'The History of the *Pharmacopoeia Londinensis*' and a facsimile of the first issue.

Van Wyk, B.-E., Van Oudtshoorn, B. and Gericke, N., *Medicinal plants of South Africa,* Pretoria, South Africa, Briza Publications, 2000.

Winter, J.C., *Tobacco use by Native Americans: Sacred smoke and silent killer,* University of Oklahoma Press, 2000.

Withering, W., *An Account of the Foxglove*, Birmingham, M. Swinney for G.G.J. and J. Robinson, London, 1785.

Woodville, W., *Medical Botany* vol. 1–3, London, James Phillips, 1790–93.

More information on the plants in the Medicinal Garden of the College can be found at http://garden.rcplondon.ac.uk and http://www.rcplondon.ac.uk/museum-and-garden/garden/